UNDERSTANDING
BELIEFS

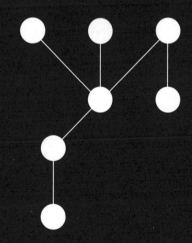

The MIT Press Essential Knowledge Series

Understanding Beliefs, Nils J. Nilsson
Computing: A Concise History, Paul Ceruzzi
Crowdsourcing, Daren C. Brabham
Free Will, Mark Balaguer
Information and the Modern Corporation, James Cortada
Intellectual Property Strategy, John Palfrey
Memes in Digital Culture, Limor Shifman
Open Access, Peter Suber
Paradox, Margaret Cuonzo
Waves, Fred Raichlen

UNDERSTANDING
BELIEFS

NILS J. NILSSON

The MIT Press | Cambridge, Massachusetts | London, England

MIT Press books may be purchased at special quantity discounts for business or sales promotional use. For information, please email special_sales @mitpress.mit.

This book was set in Chaparral Pro by the MIT Press. Printed and bound in the United States of America.

Library of Congress Cataloging-in-Publication Data

Nilsson, Nils J., 1933-
Understanding beliefs / Nils J. Nilsson.
   pages   cm
Includes bibliographical references and index.
ISBN 978-0-262-52643-2 (pbk. : alk. paper) 1. Belief and doubt. I. Title.
BD215.N55 2014
121'.6--dc23
2013047479

10 9 8 7 6 5 4 3 2 1

[Belief] … that upon which a man is prepared to act.

—Alexander Bain, psychologist, quoted in Louis Menand,
The Metaphysical Club[1]

Man's most valuable trait is a judicious sense of what not
to believe.

—Euripides, circa 480–406 BCE

We may not know very much, but we do know something,
and while we must always be prepared to change our
minds, we must act as best we can in the light of what we
do know.

—W. H. Auden, quoted in Adam Gopnik, "The Double Man"[2]

CONTENTS

Series Foreword   ix
Preface   xi
Acknowledgments   xv

1   Beliefs, Knowledge, and Models   1
2   What Do Beliefs Do for Us?   11
3   Where Do Beliefs Come From?   21
4   Evaluating Beliefs   35
5   In All Probability   51
6   Reality and Truth   65
7   The Scientific Method   75
8   Robot Beliefs   105
9   Belief Traps   117

Glossary   131
Notes   137
Further Readings   143
Index   145

SERIES FOREWORD

The MIT Press Essential Knowledge series offers accessible, concise, beautifully produced pocket-size books on topics of current interest. Written by leading thinkers, the books in this series deliver expert overviews of subjects that range from the cultural and the historical to the scientific and the technical.

In today's era of instant information gratification, we have ready access to opinions, rationalizations, and superficial descriptions. Much harder to come by is the foundational knowledge that informs a principled understanding of the world. Essential Knowledge books fill that need. Synthesizing specialized subject matter for nonspecialists and engaging critical topics through fundamentals, each of these compact volumes offers readers a point of access to complex ideas.

Bruce Tidor
Professor of Biological Engineering and Computer Science
Massachusetts Institute of Technology

PREFACE

I became interested in the subject of how people come to know things through my work in artificial intelligence and robotics. In order for robots to perform acceptably, they must know something about the worlds they inhabit. We know how robots "know" because we build them. Some of the knowledge that robots possess comes pre-installed by their designers and builders. Some comes more-or-less directly from their perceptual apparatus—what they see, read, touch, and hear. But robots can also "manufacture" additional knowledge in the form of explanations and conclusions for knowledge they already have. It's the same for us humans. Perhaps our DNA encodes some knowledge as predispositions shaped by our evolution. But the rest is built on our perceptions and on our abilities to reason and to construct theories.

Brain science hasn't progressed far enough yet for us to have a detailed picture of how we humans know things. Even so, cognitive psychologists and philosophers have had a lot to say about knowledge. Psychologists talk about different kinds of knowledge, two kinds in particular: knowing *how*, which they call "procedural," and knowing *that*, which they call "declarative." Knowing how to ride a bicycle is procedural—it's built into a program in the brain that enables bicycle riding. Knowing that a bicycle has two wheels is declarative—it can be stated as a declarative sentence.

The branch of philosophy concerned with the study of knowledge is called "epistemology." Philosophers distinguish *how* knowledge from *that* knowledge also. Epistemology is mainly concerned with *that* knowledge—the kind that can be represented by declarative sentences (which philosophers often call "propositions"). For example, the sentence (or proposition), "The sun is fueled by thermonuclear reactions," constitutes a piece of scientific knowledge.

But what about "beliefs"? Do our beliefs, expressed as declarative sentences, constitute "knowledge"? Even though some of our beliefs are less strongly held than others, I think the sum total of them does comprise a person's "knowledge" about the world. It's all he or she has. (In artificial intelligence, it's common to refer to a set of propositions as a "knowledge base," even when some of the propositions are uncertain.)

Some epistemologists attempt to distinguish belief from knowledge. After all, they claim, beliefs might not represent "reality" faithfully, whereas knowledge must. Because I don't think it's possible to decide whether or not a sentence (or a set of them) represents reality faithfully (whatever that might mean), I don't think it's possible to distinguish knowledge from belief in a qualitatively meaningful way. Nevertheless, many people speak as if there were a difference between believing something and knowing something. For example, I've occasionally had arguments with one of my colleagues—I'll call him Charlie—about something or other. These often ended by my saying, "I understand that you *believe* that, Charlie." Charlie would respond, poking me in the sternum, by saying "I don't *believe* it, I *know* it." Whereas Charlie thought there was a real difference between believing and knowing, to me the sternum poke simply indicated the strength of his belief.

When someone says he *knows* some proposition, I interpret that to mean that he *believes* it very, very strongly—even when I might not believe it at all. Such a person may equivalently say that a strongly held proposition is *true*. The same applies for me. I will tend to say that I *know* things that I believe quite strongly, and I will label them *true*. Because people use the word "know" for their strong beliefs, they may think (like Charlie) that the difference between knowing something and believing something involves more than just the strength of a belief. I don't think there is a way to describe what that "more" might be. Chapter 6 of this book will explore knowing and truth more thoroughly.

Many of our beliefs fall in between strong belief and disbelief. Because our beliefs influence our actions, and because some of our actions might have profound consequences, I think it is important to evaluate beliefs carefully.

Chapter 4 is devoted to methods for evaluating beliefs. I think the set of practices that has come to be called the scientific method (explored in chapter 7) offers the most helpful way to evaluate beliefs of all kinds. Like scientific theories, all of our beliefs are (or should be) subject to change.

This book describes my beliefs about beliefs. It's written for those who, like myself, are interested in forming their own beliefs about beliefs. Many of my beliefs are quite controversial, and you may disagree with them. But, after all, you can take them simply as *my* beliefs!

About the Notes

So as not to distract the general reader unnecessarily, numbered notes containing citations to source materials appear by chapter at the end of the book. (Notes for the epigraphs at the beginning of the book are listed first under the heading, "Opening Epigraphs.")

ACKNOWLEDGMENTS

Several people read many drafts of this book (including an unpublished early predecessor titled *How Are We to Know?*). All have made helpful comments, suggestions, or corrections. I'm sure that few agreed with everything or even most of what they read in the drafts. I hope I haven't left too many people out of this list: Dave Berwyn, Ike Burke, Daniel Curtis, Oscar Firschein, Michael Genesereth, Ned Hall, Peter Hart, Hugh Haskell, John Iwuc, Mykel and Mary Anne Kochenderfer, Sidney Liebes, Alan Marer, Andy Neher, Walter Nilsson, Bill Rowe, George Slinn, David Stork, Robert Voss, Yin Wang, and Andrew Waterman. Mary Bagg did an excellent job of copyediting, and I also am grateful for the suggestions of six anonymous reviewers. My thanks to all! Most especially, I want to thank my wife, Grace McConnell Abbott, who read through innumerable drafts and suggested many important improvements.

BELIEFS, KNOWLEDGE, AND MODELS

Our beliefs constitute a large part of our knowledge of the world. For example, I believe I exist on a planet that we call Earth and that I share it with billions of other people. I have beliefs about objects, such as automobiles, airplanes, computers, and various tools, and (to various degrees of detail) how they all operate. I have beliefs about the twenty-first-century culture in which I live: about democracy and the rule of law, about the Internet, and about science and the humanities, among other things. I have beliefs about many other people, including family, friends, associates, and even others yet unmet. And, I believe that they have beliefs also. To make an explicit list of all of my beliefs would be impossible. Yet, all of these beliefs are there, somewhere and somehow represented in my brain—changing, growing, shrinking, and mostly ready for use when I need them.

If I were to try to list my beliefs, I would do so using sentences in English, such as, "The universe is around 14 billion years old," "Salem is the capital of Oregon," "John Jones usually does what he says he is going to do," and so on. I can also state what I do *not* believe. For example, "I do not believe in extrasensory perception." And, I can state that I don't know something. For example, "I don't know the population of Sri Lanka."

We often refer to our beliefs (or to sets of them) as "theories." We construct theories about everyday experience—both social and personal. Why are crime rates falling in New York City? Why did Booth assassinate Lincoln? Why is my child falling behind in school? Why is unemployment so high (or so low)?

Scientific theories are proposed and argued over by scientists. There are theories to account for fossils found in rocks, for the sun's almost limitless energy, for earthquakes and volcanoes, for the diversity of life forms, for mental behavior, for the birth and death of stars, and for essentially everything else we can perceive about the universe. Usually scientific theories are described by many sentences—replete with mathematics. They are written down in articles and books to supplement what's stored in the brains of scientists. When scientists say that they "believe" in quantum mechanics, for example, they are assenting to theories contained in certain articles and books about quantum mechanics. Scientific theories usually have to pass more stringent tests than do the personal theories we all have about many things.

Besides the literature of science, nonfiction books such as histories, political analyses, biographies, and narratives purport to set forth their authors' beliefs about something. You and I might adopt some of these beliefs as our own. For example, you might say that you believe Stephen Ambrose's story about the Lewis and Clark expedition as told in his book *Undaunted Courage*. Even books of fiction contain descriptions of the world that we might incorporate into our beliefs.

One of the most important things to say about beliefs is that they are (or at least should be) tentative and changeable. For example, my belief that the weather will be sunny tomorrow (based on a weather forecast I consulted) may change as new weather data arrives. I may change some of my more fundamental beliefs also, such as my beliefs about early childhood education. Science and medicine advance by new experiments and new theoretical explanations, and these entail new or changed beliefs.

Cognitive scientists distinguish various kinds of knowledge. Knowledge represented by beliefs is called "declarative" because beliefs are stated as declarative sentences. No one really knows how beliefs are represented in our brains. The philosopher and cognitive scientist Jerry Fodor proposes that they are represented as sentence-like forms in a "language of thought" he calls "mentalese."

One of the most important things to say about beliefs is that they are (or at least should be) tentative and changeable.

Neuroscientists, psychologists, and philosophers continue to argue about whether there are any such sentence-like representations in our brains at all. For our purposes we won't worry about how beliefs are actually represented in the brain. Because we state them using sentences, it seems reasonable to think of them as sentences—constrained by the languages we use to construct sentences.

Cognitive scientists also talk about other kinds of knowledge also. One of these is called "procedural."[1] Procedural knowledge is built into our practiced actions, such as swinging a golf club or riding a bicycle. For tasks that require real-time coordination between sensing and acting, procedural knowledge is more effective than declarative knowledge would be. (After memorizing some sentences about how to do a cartwheel, could you do one?) Analogously, the knowledge that a computer system uses when it parks a car or lands a plane automatically is of this procedural sort. Most likely much of the knowledge that animals have about their world, such as how to construct spider webs, how to migrate, how to chase prey, and so on, is procedural.

Procedural knowledge is important, but it is limited to those specific actions that it enables. The main reason that we humans are so much more versatile than other animals is that a good deal of our knowledge about the world is declarative and thus can be used to guide many different actions. To use a rather mundane example, our belief that

Before we trust a belief sufficiently to act on it, we can analyze it and perhaps modify it—taking into account our own experiences, reasoning, and the opinions and criticisms of others.

exercise promotes good health can encourage us to swim, to cycle, or to jog.

Of equal importance to its utility in many different situations, declarative knowledge can be discussed and debated. Before we trust a belief sufficiently to act on it, we can analyze it and perhaps modify it—taking into account our own experiences, reasoning, and the opinions and criticisms of others. As the philosopher Karl Popper put it, "By criticizing our theories we can let our theories die in our stead."[2]

Beliefs constitute one of the ways we describe the world we live in. We also use mathematical equations (such as $E = mc^2$), computer simulations of various phenomena (such as the weather), maps, and stories. The sum total of all of these constitutes a *model* of reality—an accessible substitute for reality itself. We must make do with this substitute because we can't apprehend reality directly; it's on the other side of a "sensory curtain." Even though it's easy to imagine that the objects, properties, and relations mentioned in our beliefs actually exist as part of reality, they are only components of the declarative part of our *model* of reality—a kind of "virtual reality." As the physicist David Deutsch wrote:[3]

> Reality is out there: objective, physical and
> independent of what we believe about it. But we
> never experience that reality directly. Every last

scrap of our external experience is of virtual reality. And every last scrap of our knowledge—including our knowledge of the non-physical worlds of logic, mathematics and philosophy, and of imagination, fiction, art and fantasy—is encoded in the form of programs for the rendering of those worlds on our brain's own virtual-reality generator. … So it is not just science—reasoning about the physical world—that involves virtual reality. All reasoning, all thinking and all external experience are forms of virtual reality.

Even though virtual reality is not reality itself, it can feel very real. As the biologist and writer Richard Dawkins says, "Of course, we feel as if we are firmly placed in the real world—which is exactly as it should be if our constrained virtual reality software is any good. It is very good, and the only time we notice it at all is on the rare occasions when it gets something wrong."[4]

Here's one way to think about the virtual reality that we inhabit: Imagine a pilot flying a giant jetliner through clouds. He can see nothing outside the plane with his own eyes but must rely on the instrument panel displays, which inform him about the plane's position, speed, and relationship to the surrounding terrain. The plane is actually in the real world, of course, but all the pilot knows about it is represented in the virtual reality of the plane's meters, displays, and force-feedback mechanisms. This virtual reality is not reality itself but only a model of it. If the model is not a good one, the plane might be in danger of stalling, running out of fuel, or even colliding with a mountain top.

We are all in a situation similar to that of this airplane pilot. Our models are analogous to his instrument panel's meters and displays. Our beliefs are an important component of these models. Just as the airplane pilot wouldn't trust meters and displays that have not been thoroughly tested, we would do well not to trust beliefs that have not been rigorously evaluated.

WHAT DO BELIEFS DO FOR US?

Our beliefs serve us in several ways. Some help us make predictions and select actions, some help us understand a subject in more detail, some inspire creativity, some generate emotional responses, and some can even be self-fulfilling.

First, let's look at some of the ways people use beliefs to make predictions and select actions. In medicine, for example, physicians use their beliefs (learned in medical school and from journals, clinical studies, and on-the-job practice) to diagnose and predict the course of a disease and to prescribe a therapy predicted to cure or mitigate it. Corporate CEOs use their beliefs about business practices to predict the likely results of new strategies, capital allocations, reorganizations, and other actions that might be taken. Attorneys use their beliefs about torts, about the client, about precedents, and about the surrounding circumstances to devise a strategy for trying an injury case.

In everyday life, we all make belief-based predictions. For example, if we believe that John Jones keeps his appointments, we can confidently predict that he will be there to meet us at the time and place he specified (*which* time and place, incidentally, are also represented as beliefs). Or, if we believe a radio traffic report that our usual route to work is congested, we can predict that we will be delayed unless we choose a different route.

More significantly, our beliefs help us make decisions about education, career choice, mate selection, child rearing, health practices, family finances, friendships, ethics, voting, and many other aspects of our personal lives. Actions evoked by these beliefs can have profound consequences, both beneficial and harmful. Consider, for example, the different consequences resulting from a physician's belief that certain antibiotics can cure bacterial pneumonia contrasted with those resulting from a shaman's belief that pneumonia can be cured by magical incantations. We have the opportunity and, I think, the duty to scrutinize our beliefs carefully.

How do our beliefs affect our actions? Sometimes they don't, at least not consciously. We seem to have many pre-stored, habitual routines (procedural knowledge) for dealing with daily life. We drive our automobiles, run errands, and even engage in conversations largely on "auto-pilot." Someone says something to us, and we frequently react without thinking. In these situations, we are doing what the psychologist Daniel Kahneman calls "fast thinking."[1] Kahneman, who won a Nobel Prize for his work on behavioral economics, suggests that our brains have two very different ways of thinking. One, which he calls "System 1," does fast thinking. It uses built-in pattern recognition abilities, habits, and stored experiences to make rapid decisions. System 1 controls many of our routine, daily activities. "System 2," on the other hand, thinks more slowly. Its conclusions are arrived at by the deliberate use of whatever analytical and reasoning tools we happen to possess.

Kahneman gives the following example to show the difference between the two systems: "A bat and ball costs $1.10. The bat costs one dollar more than the ball. How much does the ball cost?" Many people come up with a fast answer, 10 cents, using System 1. But that's wrong! To do the math and find the correct answer, which is 5 cents, one needs to use System 2. Kahneman's book gives several other examples. For many situations, especially those in which a fast decision is required, fast thinking provides useable advice. It's a good thing too, because trying to use slow thinking methods *all the time* would paralyze us into inaction. But in less time-critical, high-stakes situations, fast thinking can lead us dangerously astray, and we should be thinking much more slowly and carefully.

Here's how slow and careful thinking might work to choose an action based on beliefs. First, the current situation is perceived. Next, the most appropriate goal-achieving actions that can be taken in that situation are identified and their likely effects are predicted. Finally, the action that leads to the most desirable effects is selected. Our beliefs play important roles in perceiving a current situation, in identifying appropriate actions, and in predicting the effects of these actions. As I will note in chapter 3, what we perceive is highly dependent on our belief-dependent expectations. And, what we expect to be the results of an action depends on our beliefs about how the world works. Because beliefs play such an important role in action selection, thorough and systematic methods should be used to evaluate beliefs, especially in critical situations. Describing these methods is the main focus of chapter 4.

Another thing that beliefs do for us (besides their role in action selection) is to help us explain what we observe. For example, long experience evokes the belief that in the earth's temperate zones, it is generally colder during some parts of the year, the parts we call winter, than it is during the other parts, called summer. This belief *explains* previous observations, makes predictions about subsequent observations, and prompts us to take preparatory actions. However, it turns out that we are constitutionally unable to leave it at that—we seek and must have deeper explanations. *Why* is it colder in winter than in summer? A first attempt at an explanation might be that the sun is lower in the sky during the winter than it is during the summer. Thus, the earth's temperate zones receive less heat

Our beliefs play important roles in perceiving a current situation, in identifying appropriate actions, and in predicting the effects of these actions.

in winter than they do in summer and that explains why winter is colder than summer. But why this odd behavior of the sun? Primitive peoples probably had their explanations. Perhaps one of their gods arranged it to be so. Modern knowledge has a more satisfactory explanation: The tilt of the earth's axis results in a change of the angle of the midday sun relative to places on earth as the earth traverses its orbit. Why does the earth's axis tilt? Scientists have explanations for that also. Each level of belief gives us additional *understanding*. Beliefs gain credibility if they are explained by other beliefs having high credibility.

We sometimes think of an explanatory belief as describing the *cause* of that which is explained. Thus, we might say that the tilt of the earth's axis causes it to be colder in winter than in summer. In addition to our evolved ability to have beliefs in the first place, we also have evolved a compelling need to seek explanations or causes for the things we believe. Science is all about inventing explanations or causes for things we observe. So is mythology, for that matter. The main difference between the two is that science is concerned with subjecting its explanations to rigorous testing and analysis, whereas mythology is not.

Scientific beliefs usually involve a deep hierarchy of beliefs. Each belief in the hierarchy is an explanation for the beliefs immediately above it and follows from the explanation below it. For example, the belief that the earth and its sister planets travel around the sun in elliptical orbits can be explained by Newton's laws of motion and gravity. Newton explained gravity by imagining a force that acts between masses. More recently, Einstein explained gravity by postulating a curved space-time. Scientists are still seeking a deeper explanation for gravity, one that is consistent with quantum mechanics. Some physicists think they have found such an explanation in string theory.

Explanations frequently cross scientific disciplines. For example, complex biological processes can be explained by chemical and mechanical reactions, which in turn are grounded in physics. The process of explaining scientific theories by more detailed theories is often called "reductionism." Because that word is sometimes misunderstood to imply that something is lost in the explanation, I prefer the term "explanationism."

Besides helping us to make useful predictions and to achieve greater depths of understanding, some beliefs can evoke profound emotional and creative responses. Religious and aesthetic beliefs continue to inspire great art, music, literature, and poetry, and to move us with awe and wonder. So do scientific beliefs, many of which overwhelm the imagination. The Big Bang gave rise to billions and billions of galaxies, which are now moving farther and farther apart at unimaginable speeds and distances. Over vast amounts of time, the processes of selective survival of organisms coded by DNA (itself a wonder), together with random changes and shuffling in DNA, produced all the infinitely varied and amazing life forms on the earth.

Keats, perhaps blind to the possibilities for scientific knowledge to inspire awe, complained in his poem "Lamia" that Newton's scientific experiments with the prism had destroyed the poetry of the rainbow. But an understanding of how sunlight and water droplets actually create a rainbow can, as Richard Dawkins observed, inspire its own poetry.[2] The physicist Richard Feynman, commenting on the beauty of science, once said, "It only adds. I don't understand how it subtracts."

Beliefs also have entertainment value. When we see a play, for example, we are able to "suspend disbelief" temporarily in order to immerse ourselves in the action.

Some beliefs just make us feel good, and that's one reason people hold them. That rationale for belief is called *credo consolans* (i.e., I believe because it is comforting). Some believe in life after death. Some believe that they have personal angels who look after them. Many believe there is a God who directs their lives. Such beliefs, in my opinion, are fairy tales, but fairy tales can be quite seductive, as the following song lyrics proclaim:[3]

> Truth is hard and tough as nails,
> That's why we need fairy tales.
> I'm all through with logical conclusions,
> Why should I deny myself illusions?

We use beliefs to predict, to explain, to create, to inspire, to be entertained, to feel good, and to buttress confidence.

The economist Robin Hanson has an interesting analogy about beliefs. He says that the beliefs people hold are like the clothes they wear.[4] People wear clothes for a variety of reasons—for the strictly utilitarian reason to keep warm, of course. But they also choose clothes because they are fashionable, because they feel good, or because they are the clothes that they just happen to have. It's the same with beliefs, although I think we should think more carefully about our beliefs than we do about our clothes. In particular, we shouldn't necessarily accept beliefs just because they make us feel good. Likewise, we shouldn't necessarily reject ones that make us feel bad.

Just as clothes can influence our self-image, so can beliefs. The very act of believing in our ability to do something can influence that ability and thus be self-fulfilling. There's a saying that goes, "Whether you believe you can or believe you cannot, you're probably right." Self-confidence, even when initially unjustified, can be a powerful force for success.

In summary, we use beliefs to predict, to explain, to create, to inspire, to be entertained, to feel good, and to buttress confidence. Our beliefs are an important part of what makes us human. But, where do we get these beliefs? That's the subject of the next chapter.

WHERE DO BELIEFS COME FROM?

Have you ever asked yourself, "Where did I get that belief?" or "Why do I believe that?" Sometimes we can give answers to such questions. "I saw it with my own eyes." "I learned it in school." "I read it in the *Wall Street Journal*." "I heard it on TV." "My parents told me." "I found it on the Internet." Sometimes we aren't sure and have to say something like, "I don't know; it just seems right to me."

Interestingly, the anthropologist David Fleck describes a language spoken in Amazonian Peru and Brazil that requires "speakers to precisely and explicitly code their source of information every time they report a past event."[1] For example, Fleck writes, one cannot simply say in that language, "A non-Indian passed by" and leave it at that. Instead, the grammar required for stating such reports forces one to say something like, "A non-Indian passed by, according to my father, who heard about it from my grandfather, who in turn heard about it from Tumi."

Even though our own language does not require us to be explicit about the sources of our beliefs, they all *do* have sources. We aren't born with our beliefs. We get beliefs in two main ways: first, from all of our senses, especially by seeing, hearing, touching, and reading; and second, by inventing explanations for and deriving consequences from what we already believe. As small children, we infer the existence of objects and construct beliefs about them to explain our earliest sensations. As adults, we continue to pile beliefs upon beliefs to explain all the new things we observe, including what we hear and read.

Regardless of what Plato might have thought, there is no way that our minds have direct access to "eternal truths." Our senses, especially vision, hearing, and touch, are our only portals to reality. Indispensable as they are, however, our senses can also mislead us. Vision provides some good examples. "Seeing is believing," but what we see doesn't always produce a reliable belief. Errors can arise because what we think we see is influenced by what we already believe. We often "see" what we expect to see, and don't see what we don't anticipate. In a famous 1949 experiment, the psychologists Jerome Bruner and Leo Postman presented quick glimpses of pictures of trick playing cards to a group of subjects.[2] Quite often the subjects said that a black three of hearts, for example, was either a normal three of spades (misperceiving the heart for a spade) or a normal three of hearts (misperceiving the black color for red). Expectations about the playing cards interfered with accurate perception.

Eyewitness reports at crime scenes, often used in court proceedings, are another example. They are notoriously unreliable, being influenced, as they are, by misperceptions and mis-remembrances. In fact, the New Jersey Supreme Court recently issued instructions for judges to give jurors about evaluating evidence provided by eyewitnesses. According to a *New York Times* report:[3]

> A judge now must tell jurors before deliberations begin that, for example, stress levels, distance or poor lighting can undercut an eyewitness's ability to make an accurate identification.
>
> Factors like the time that has elapsed between the commission of a crime and a witness's identification of a suspect or the behavior of a police officer during a lineup can also influence a witness, the new instructions warn.

Visual perception attempts to extract three-dimensional information from the two-dimensional images gathered by each one of our eyes. That can only be done if our models of the world—informing our expectations—supply the missing information. Usually, the process works amazingly well, but there are many well-known visual illusions caused by expectations.

Figure 1 shows an interesting example of a visual illusion. Are the two tables really different? They appear to be because we interpret them as tables in three dimensions. But what about the *two-dimensional* figures representing the tabletops? If you actually measure their dimensions on the page, you will see that one is just a rotated version of the other. (Roger Shepard, the psychologist who created this experiment in illusion, called it "turning-the-tables.") Our propensity to see the picture as a representation of a three-dimensional scene overwhelms any attempt to perceive the figures in two dimensions. Compelling expectations can cause perceptual errors.

Even reliable perception doesn't always give us a good description of reality because things are not always what they appear to be. The earth appears flat—except for the bumps of hills and valleys—as early humans thought it to be. And the sun appears to move through the sky. In these cases, and in many others, we need a model other than the one directly constructed by our sensory apparatus. One of the Beatles' songs describes the difference between what our eyes report and what we construct as a mental image:[4]

... the fool on the hill,
Sees the sun going down,
And the eyes in his head,
See the world spinning 'round.

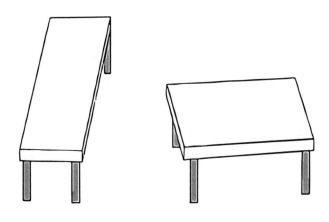

Figure 1 Two tables

These days, much of what we sense comes to us through language. Our eyes see written texts of all kinds—books, newspapers, articles, scientific papers, and Web pages. Our ears hear what people say to us—people talking directly to us, such as parents, friends, teachers, salespeople, clerks, and so on. We also hear people talking on the radio and television. Combined video and audio media such as movies, television, and the Internet flood both our eyes and ears, and the brain behind them.

There are people who believe we have ways of getting information about reality other than through the usual sensory channels of seeing, hearing, and so on. The idea that there are extrasensory ways of perceiving "truths" is actually quite common. Every age has had mystics who claimed to hear voices revealing eternal truths. It's not unusual for people to say something like, "I know in my heart that it's true." It's as if an internal "truth bell" rings loudly for some beliefs—when it rings, its owner experiences an intense feeling that that belief *must* be true. In mental diseases, such as paranoia, the truth bell rings for beliefs that are completely disconnected from reality, beliefs that someone is "out to get me," for example.

Even some scientists claim to have inner feelings about the truth of something or other. The physicist Roger Penrose thinks that some humans have a built-in ability to perceive mathematical truths directly. He believes that mathematical quantities, like π, or numbers like 0 and 1, *exist* out in the world and are there to be *perceived* by those capable of doing so. Many mathematicians say they have a powerful feeling that certain propositions just *must* be true. And, there are physicists who say that certain theories are "too beautiful not to be true." Perhaps to be a good mathematician or physicist, the impact of ideas must be so intense that it's as if these ideas *were* actually out there, waiting to be discovered. However, rather than coming to us through extrasensory means, I think that those beliefs that we "know in our hearts are true" are actually mental constructions composed of parts of already existing ideas strung together by our creative and reasoning processes.

All of our beliefs are mental constructions. Some are *consequences* of other beliefs, and some are *explanations* built to explain existing beliefs and experiences. Let's consider each of these types in turn.

First, *consequences*. Many of our beliefs entail others—constructed by logical reasoning. Trial lawyers often use this mode of reasoning. For example, if the accused, let's call him Sam Brown, is believed not to have been at the scene of the crime when it occurred, and if the jury can be persuaded that the perpetrator of this kind of crime *had* to be at the scene, then the jury can conclude that Sam Brown is not guilty. (Or so the defense attorney hopes.) Of course, we don't always draw consequences from our beliefs, and we never draw *all* of them. Arguing about beliefs often involves getting a person to see what his beliefs entail. The

All of our beliefs are mental constructions. Some are *consequences* of other beliefs, and some are *explanations* built to explain existing beliefs and experiences.

so-called Socratic method uses this style to tease out beliefs that are, in some sense, already there.

It is important to realize, however, that logical deductions can never give us any really new beliefs that are independent of those we already have. The subject of geometry provides an interesting example. Early geometers and philosophers believed that purely by *thinking* they could establish geometric facts about the world. But all such thinking did was to derive consequences implicit in the axioms of Euclidean geometry. Astronomical observations, not logic, were needed before modern physics could come up with axioms that describe the universe more accurately than did those of Euclid.

What about the other type of beliefs, namely *explanations*? We construct explanations as possible answers to *why* we believe something. Why do I believe Tom will repay the loan I made to him? Because I believe he is trustworthy. We construct explanations largely by a process of inquiring, "From what beliefs would the explained belief follow?"—in other words, by an attempt to use something like logic "in reverse." Whereas logical conclusions from a set of beliefs cannot, by the nature of logic, be any more or less suspect than are the beliefs from which they were drawn, explanations are always suspect and need to be critically examined before being adopted.

One way to create an explanation is to generalize from a specific experience. For example, a child nipped by an over-eager pet dog certainly believes he was bitten, and he might form the explanatory belief "all dogs bite." That new belief explains why he was bitten. But, of course, it isn't a very good explanation.

Some explanations involve beliefs about what causes what, such as turning on a light switch *causes* the light to shine. Why is the light on? Someone must have turned on the light switch. Causal beliefs are often formed by noting the proximity of events in time. For example, if we happen to observe that event A is followed by event B, we are likely to adopt the belief that A causes B. Beginning even in early childhood, we form beliefs about the physical world from these kinds of observations. Dropping a raw egg on a hard floor leads to it breaking open. Does that always happen? If so, we have a new belief about eggs.[5] A special sensitivity to temporal sequences of events was probably programmed into us through evolution. The flow of events helps us develop beliefs about how we can predict and affect that flow.

Of course, the proximity of two events in time doesn't always mean that the first event caused the second. They might both be caused by some earlier third event. Or their closeness in time might just be a coincidence. Such coincidences are the source of many superstitions. For example, if a baseball pitcher observes that he wore his cap a certain way while having a good run of strike-outs, he might think it to be a cause of his success and insist on wearing it that way even through a run of bad pitches. Superstitions are surprisingly robust.

The details of the processes by which our brains actually construct explanations are subjects for neuropsychology and neuroscience. But so far, we don't really know very much about those processes, even though progress is being made. But we do know that explanations can only be constructed from the materials at hand—that is, from whatever beliefs and concepts that happen to be around. Explanations involve the use of objects, their properties, and the relations among them that are already in our models. Thor hurling thunderbolts was an early explanation for lightning and thunder. Nowadays we explain them by the discharge of static electricity and the sound waves these discharges create. Thor, thunderbolts, static electricity, and sound waves are all mental objects we have invented. The materials primitive peoples had available were quite limited, but they constructed explanations anyway—many that we see today as myths and fanciful stories. People in the future may think that the materials we use now for explanations were rather limited also.

People have a wired-in need and ability to construct and reconstruct models for describing their world. We are extraordinarily creative at constructing theories. Ideas such as astrology, extrasensory perception, guardian angels, communication with the dead, auras, reincarnation, the lost continent of Atlantis, alien abduction, and

We do know that explanations can only be constructed from the materials at hand—that is, from whatever beliefs and concepts that happen to be around.

"energy" flow in the body are quite imaginative if not very believable to the twenty-first-century scientific mind. Equally imaginative, and perhaps more believable, are current theories in physics and biology, such as those of quantum mechanics, evolution, the Big Bang and cosmic "inflation," general relativity, and protein folding. All of these display the fruits of fertile brains attempting to create explanations. The important thing is whether or not we should believe the explanations that we hear about or that we create ourselves. That's a topic I'll deal with in the next chapter.

EVALUATING BELIEFS

We hold some of our beliefs more strongly than others. If asked whether we believe such and such, we might answer by saying things like, "Yes, definitely, it's a fact," or "It's quite likely to be so," or "It's possible," or "It's doubtful," or "I don't know," or "Not at all." These are some of the ways of describing degrees of belief. No one knows how our brains actually represent belief strengths. Perhaps we store some of them as sentences such as "I doubt that vitamin C can cure a cold." Or, maybe our brains associate something like numbers with beliefs to indicate their strengths. But regardless of what is going on in our brains, we are able to state how credible we think a belief is. And (with some effort), we are able to change the credibility of a belief by considering evidence for and against it.

As I mentioned in the preface, when we believe something very, very strongly, we typically say we "know" it, and that it's a "fact." For example, "At the present time, I live in Oregon." I call that belief of mine a fact, and I say that I know it. "George Washington was the first president of the United States," and that belief of mine is also a fact. Just because someone claims he knows something, however, doesn't mean I would necessarily agree with him. Furthermore, his belief might even change someday if confronted by new evidence. The author Sam Arbesman claims that many of the beliefs that we label as "facts" have what he calls a "half-life," after which they cease to be facts.[1] For example, doctors once thought it to be a fact that malaria was caused by the "bad air" in swamps and marshes, but they don't believe that anymore because a micro-organism spread by infected mosquitoes is a better explanation.

How do we decide to say of some beliefs that we know them and that others are only likely? There are several ways in which people decide about the strengths of beliefs. Any method for evaluating beliefs is faced with a trade-off. If our criteria for belief acceptance are too strict, we are likely to exclude some useful beliefs. Missing out on useful beliefs is the price we pay for extreme skepticism. On the other hand, if we want to be sure that we do not exclude useful beliefs, we are likely to accept many questionable, even useless or harmful ones as well. Accepting bad beliefs is the price we pay for extreme credulity.

Some people are quite credulous, willing to believe almost anything, especially if the belief sounds fascinating or just makes them feel good. Others are very skeptical, with a "show me, I'm from Missouri" attitude. Scientists usually operate toward the skeptical end of this spectrum. Whether credulous or skeptical, some judge a belief on whether or not it "feels right." The sense of feeling right might be caused by certain brain processes, which while perhaps unconscious, might nevertheless be taking account of many other related and strongly held beliefs. These processes are probably the basis of what we call "intuition." But because missing out on useful beliefs or accepting bad ones can have life-altering consequences, we should back up our intuitions about beliefs with more disciplined, critical thinking—slow thinking, as Daniel Kahneman calls it.

As young children we usually believe quite strongly what our parents and teachers tell us. After all, the beliefs passed down by our parents might well have had survival value. But parents, along with everyone else, might believe a lot of nonsense. As young children, we haven't yet been exposed to a wide range of alternative beliefs. Such exposure, along with critical thinking, is necessary before we can jettison some of the beliefs of our parents and elders. Doing so often takes an act of conscious will.

What are the elements of critical thinking? Suppose we are considering some proposition as a possible belief—perhaps one we read or heard about. How would we evaluate it? To illustrate, let's consider, for example, the proposition that the earth is warming. Because a warming

Because missing out on useful beliefs or accepting bad ones can have life-altering consequences, we should back up our intuitions about beliefs with more disciplined, critical thinking.

earth would have great effects on our future, it's important to think critically about its possibility.

The first step in critical thinking is to seek the opinions of experts. Are there experts who believe that the earth is warming, and do they know enough about the subject for us to trust their judgment? In fact, there are such experts. Many of them are on the Intergovernmental Panel on Climate Change (IPCC), the leading international body for the assessment of climate change. To quote from the IPCC website, "It was established by the United Nations Environment Programme (UNEP) and the World Meteorological Organization (WMO) to provide the world with a clear scientific view on the current state of knowledge in climate change and its potential environmental and socio-economic impacts."[2] One of the IPCC's main activities "is the preparation of comprehensive assessment reports about the state of scientific, technical and socioeconomic knowledge on climate change, its causes, potential impacts and response strategies." Its main findings have been published in four multivolume reports.[3] The latest one, issued in 2007, summarized the situation as follows:[4]

> Warming of the climate system is unequivocal, as is now evident from observations of increases in global average air and ocean temperatures, widespread melting of snow and ice and rising global average sea level.

Additionally, as a National Aeronautics and Space Administration (NASA) document prepared by experts on climate concludes: "All three major global surface temperature reconstructions show that Earth has warmed since 1880. Most of this warming has occurred since the 1970s, with the 20 warmest years having occurred since 1981 and with all 10 of the warmest years occurring in the past 12 years. . . . The oceans have absorbed much of this increased heat, with the top 700 meters (about 2,300 feet) of ocean showing warming of 0.302 degrees Fahrenheit since 1969."[5]

There are even some experts who were originally skeptical about global warming, but are now convinced that it is happening. For example, Richard A. Muller, a physicist and climate scientist at the University of California, Berkeley, recently wrote:[6]

> Three years ago I identified problems in previous climate studies that, in my mind, threw doubt on the very existence of global warming. Last year, following an intensive research effort involving a dozen scientists, I concluded that global warming was real and that the prior estimates of the rate of warming were correct. I'm now going a step further: Humans are almost entirely the cause.

That's good enough for me. I agree with the philosopher Bertrand Russell who wrote, "The opinion of experts, when it is unanimous, must be accepted by non-experts as more likely to be right than the opposite opinion."[7] In sampling expert opinion, however, one has to be aware that even experts can disagree with each other. That's why Russell advises accepting the opinion of experts only if it is unanimous. And, even then, the experts might be mistaken and change their minds as new information becomes available.

The next steps of critical thinking are to consider the consequences of and the explanations for a belief. In rendering their opinion about global warming, the IPCC analyzed in great detail its consequences and explanations. Let's consider the consequences of global warming first. Recall that the consequences of a belief (or of a set of beliefs) are those propositions that would follow from it. A belief is rendered more credible if its consequences are credible (unless there are other credible explanations for those consequences). The IPCC reports mention many consequences of global warming, including "widespread melting of snow and ice and rising global average sea level." What about those consequences? Are they happening? The NASA document cited earlier summarizes, among others, these three:[8]

1. "Data from NASA's Gravity Recovery and Climate Experiment show Greenland lost 150 to 250 cubic kilometers (36 to 60 cubic miles) of ice per year between 2002 and 2006, while Antarctica lost about

152 cubic kilometers (36 cubic miles) of ice between 2002 and 2005. . . . Glaciers are retreating almost everywhere around the world—including in the Alps, Himalayas, Andes, Rockies, Alaska and Africa."
2. "Both the extent and thickness of Arctic sea ice has declined rapidly over the last several decades."
3. "Global sea level rose about 17 centimeters (6.7 inches) in the last century. The rate in the last decade, however, is nearly double that of the last century."

The conclusion that global warming is indeed happening is strengthened by the fact that all of these consequences have been confirmed.

Now let's turn to whether or not there are credible explanations for global warming. A credible explanation for a belief helps to make the belief itself more credible. Here are two possible explanations for global warming:

1. Increased heat radiation from the sun.

2. Increased retention of heat by the earth's atmosphere.

Is either of these explanations credible? According to experts, the sun's radiance does go through various periodic cycles, but the magnitudes of these cycles are too small to cause the observed increases in temperature. So we can eliminate that explanation.

What about increased retention of heat by the earth's atmosphere? It happens that heat retention has its own explanation, namely increased concentrations of carbon dioxide (CO_2), a "greenhouse gas." Scientists have established that carbon dioxide, together with some other gases, allows heat from the sun to penetrate the atmosphere but prevents it from escaping back into space—much like glass traps heat inside a greenhouse. If the levels of carbon dioxide are indeed increasing, that increase would help explain (and thus help to confirm) that the atmosphere is retaining heat, which helps to explain (and thus helps to confirm) global warming. Indeed, atmospheric CO_2 has been increasing over the past 150 years, and this increase is roughly correlated with the increase in average global temperature.

All the propositions in this global-warming example can be assembled in a network of beliefs. Such a network is illustrated in figure 2. Each belief in the network can be thought of as either a consequence of the beliefs below it and/or an explanation for the beliefs above it. The credibility of each belief in the network influences the credibilities of all of the others. Credible consequences of and explanations for a belief add "points," as it were, to the strength of that belief.

Interestingly, our global warming network can be extended in both directions. For example, one expected consequence of rising air temperatures is earlier springtime

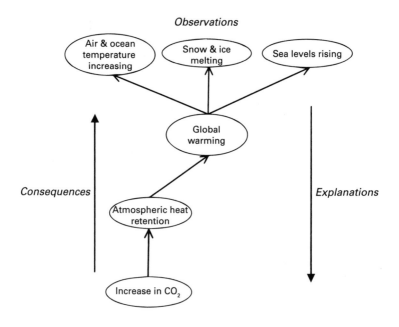

Observations

Air & ocean temperature increasing

Snow & ice melting

Sea levels rising

Global warming

Consequences

Explanations

Atmospheric heat retention

Increase in CO_2

Figure 2 A network of beliefs

budding of deciduous trees in temperate zones. Indeed, this phenomenon has been observed. And one explanation for the increasing levels of CO_2 is the increased burning of fossil fuels, which has been occurring since the industrial revolution. Factories, automobiles, heating and cooling systems, and electric power generation facilities release sufficient CO_2 to account for its increased concentration in the atmosphere. This explanation has led to the IPCC's conclusion that "most of the observed increase in global average temperatures since the mid-20th century is *very likely* due to the observed increase in anthropogenic [human-caused] greenhouse gas concentrations."

People who argue against global warming attempt to weaken the credibilities of the various pieces of evidence in its favor. For example, some claim that the atmospheric and ocean temperature readings and reconstructions are faulty. And, to argue against a belief that global warming is anthropogenic, some people have claimed that the observed increase in CO_2 is being caused by volcanic eruptions, not by the burning of fossil fuels. Offering a credible alternative explanation for a belief can weaken a competitive explanation. This strategy of argument is called "explaining away." It is used quite often in the back-and-forth of debates about beliefs. But volcanic eruptions fail to explain away fossil fuel burning as the explanation for increased CO_2 concentrations. Scientists have established that "the anthropogenic CO_2 emission rate is more than a hundred times greater than the global volcanic CO_2 emission rate."[9]

All of these elements of critical thinking—testing consequences, creating explanations, and explaining away—are mental activities that people, even children, naturally use all the time. For example, a child who initially formed the belief that all dogs bite, might (if she were adventurous) discard that belief after petting other dogs without experiencing the predicted bite. Young children who originally believed in Santa Claus explain away the belief by learning that parents are responsible for Christmas gifts. Employing these processes in a disciplined manor, however, takes more deliberate effort than most people usually exert. It takes slow thinking, as Daniel Kahneman might say.

Professional people, however, are usually quite rigorous when they use these styles of reasoning. For example, when physicians attempt to diagnose the cause of a patient's presenting symptoms, they look for diseases known to explain those symptoms. For example, if the presenting symptoms are fever and headache, a physician might suspect that the patient has a case of the flu. If it were the flu, additional common symptoms would be muscle aches and chills. Finding those symptoms in the patient would strengthen a diagnosis of flu. But these same symptoms might also indicate some variety of pneumonia. A physician would then check for pneumonia symptoms by listening to the chest and, perhaps, ordering chest x-rays. Failing to find any pneumonia symptoms would let the physician rule out that disease.

Scientists also use these very processes, in the specific and exacting ways of science, to evaluate theories. Checking to see if the predicted consequences of a theory are confirmed is an important part of all science. Confirmations of the predictions of a theory by several independent experiments or observations combine to increase confidence in the theory. And, failure of repeated experiments to confirm a prediction made by a theory would overturn that theory (or at least weaken belief in it). The explaining-away strategy is commonly used by scientists when they reject one theory in favor of another. For example, the theory of evolution, itself convincingly supported by several independent strands of evidence, is fully adequate to account for the astounding complexity of all life forms on the earth (including us). It thus explains away creation myths, such as "intelligent design." These reasoning strategies are important aspects of what is called the "scientific method," a subject that I will describe in more detail in chapter 7.

If we were to examine the relationships among *all* of our beliefs carefully, an impossible task in practice but one that is interesting to think about, we would see that some of them should make others more credible and some less. They would even compete among themselves with conflicting influences. We can imagine all of the beliefs in our large network of beliefs "fighting it out" to agree finally on the strength of each belief in the network. When they do finally agree, we say that the beliefs *cohere*. Checking for coherence in belief networks containing millions upon millions of related beliefs would be impossible. All we can hope to do, when thinking critically, is to ensure that a relatively small, circumscribed set of our beliefs is locally coherent. As we discuss our beliefs and compare them with those of others, the boundaries of local regions gradually expand, allowing more global checks on coherence. That's the principal advantage of discussing and criticizing our beliefs. Karl Popper has written:

> There is only one element of rationality in our attempts to know the world: it is the critical examination of our theories. These theories themselves are guesswork. We do not know, we only guess. If you ask me, "How do you know?" my reply would be, "I don't; I only propose a guess. If you are interested in my problem, I shall be most happy if you criticize my guess, and if you offer counterproposals, I in turn will try to criticize them."[10]

On many things, our minds are made up. But they can only stay made up if we never challenge them with new experiences, new information, and discussions with knowledgeable people who might hold opposite beliefs. These

On many things, our minds are made up. But they can only stay made up if we never challenge them with new experiences, new information, and discussions with knowledgeable people who might hold opposite beliefs.

challenges present occasions for employing the elements of critical thinking described in this chapter. In summary, they are: seeking the opinions of experts, considering the consequences of and the explanations for beliefs, and eliminating suspect explanations that can be explained away by more credible alternative ones. Changing our minds is difficult, but it is necessary if we want to have ever-more-useful descriptions of reality.

IN ALL PROBABILITY

Many of our beliefs fall somewhere between the two extremes of "definitely false" and "definitely true." Their position on that scale is indicated by what I have called a "strength." To represent these strengths, we could use phrases, such as "almost certainly not," "unlikely," "possible," "somewhat likely," "likely," "very likely," or "virtually certain." Or, we could use numbers between 0 (standing for definitely false) and 1 (standing for definitely true). It's relatively easy to convert phrases about strength into numbers. For example, we might translate "virtually certain," into 0.99 and "likely" into 0.7.

Using numbers to represent strengths reminds us of the probability numbers used by statisticians and others in dealing with uncertainty. Health scientists use probabilities when assessing the likelihoods of various diagnoses and the efficacies of treatments. Insurance underwriters use probabilities to take into account the likelihoods of losses and other events in order to establish premium rates. And, of course, we are all familiar with a weather forecaster saying the probability of rain tomorrow is 70 percent. Most statisticians claim that probability theory is the only mathematically rigorous way to deal with uncertainty. Let's take their advice and use probabilities to represent the strengths of beliefs. Probability theory is especially useful for updating the strengths of beliefs based on evidence. In this chapter, I'll summarize some basic facts about probabilities and indicate how probability theory can be used to update belief strengths.

Probability values are always numbers between 0 and 1. (Sometimes they are expressed as percentages between 0 and 100.) When we are completely certain that a proposition is true, we would give it a probability value of 1. When we are completely certain that a proposition is false, we would give it a probability value of 0. If we are uncertain about a proposition, its probability value would lie somewhere between 0 and 1.

The probability values of some propositions are constrained by those of related ones. For example, suppose I believe that there are only three people who might actually have written *The Merchant of Venice*, namely Shakespeare, Jonson, or Marlowe. Further, suppose that one, and only one, of them must have written it. These three cases are said to be "mutually exclusive and exhaustive." The probabilities of mutually exclusive and exhaustive propositions must sum to 1. So, if I am certain that Shakespeare wrote the play, then I must also be certain that neither Jonson nor Marlowe did. Of course, I could be uncertain, and believe that Shakespeare wrote it with probability 0.85, that Jonson did with probability 0.05, and that Marlowe did with probability 0.10.

Sometimes probabilities are expressed as "odds." If the odds on a belief are 4 to 1 in favor, then the probability of that belief is 0.8 or 80 percent, and the probability of its opposite is 0.2 or 20 percent. The odds are obtained by dividing 80 by 20. In sports events, such as football, the odds are sometimes estimated by experts who review past team performances and other possibly relevant factors such as weather and player injuries. All of this information is combined into a judgment they make about the odds.

Quoting the odds or the probability of a belief prepares us to place a bet on that belief. Looked at in this way, a belief is a bet that future observations will result in winning the bet. Beliefs are bets on the future.[1] When we buy a share in a company, we believe that its price will rise, and we are making a bet on that belief. When an insurance company accepts a premium from you against a fire loss on your house, it believes that your house won't burn and is making a bet on that belief. When we travel on an airplane, we believe (and bet with our lives) that the plane will not crash.

There are two major ways to assign probabilities to beliefs. The most obvious method involves collecting statistics about a large number of cases. Suppose, for example, that during the last hundred years, it rained four times in Pasadena on New Years Day. Then the probability of rain in Pasadena on New Years Day next year could be guessed to be about 4/100 or 0.04. This version of assigning probabilities to events is called the "frequency method." It's commonly used in many situations for which it's possible to collect a lot of data. For example, in 2006 the National Transportation Safety Board calculated that there are only 1.7 deaths per hundred million miles for travel by air. We use data like that to decide that it's safe to travel on airplanes.

When there isn't sufficient data to use the frequency method, we can still make an informed guess. For example, in 1999, a U.S. Geological Survey report estimated the probability of one or more large earthquakes in the San Francisco Bay Region in the next thirty years to be 0.70.[2] Guesses like these, based on expert judgment, are called "subjective probabilities." For most of the beliefs about which we are somewhat uncertain, and for which there is inadequate data, about the best we can do is make subjective probability estimates.

Rather than rely on one's own judgment to make a probability estimate, one can use the combined judgments of a pool of people. One familiar example of exploiting this kind of "crowd wisdom" is a parimutuel system for calculating the probabilities that particular horses will win a race. Using that system, several people place bets using initial probabilities provided by an expert. The results of all of these bets are used continuously, as they are made, to update the probabilities. In a three-horse race, for example, if there is a total of $3,000 so far bet on Silky, $4,000 bet on Stewball, and $3,000 bet on Scramble (all to win), then the estimated probabilities of winning will be 0.3 each for Silky and Scramble, and 0.4 for Stewball. These estimates are then used to calculate the payoffs of winning: 7 to 3 each for Silky and for Scramble, and 6 to 4 for Stewball.

Another method of pooling judgments to arrive at subjective probabilities is based on markets. People can use these markets to place bets on the outcome of certain events by buying or selling "contracts." The prices of the contracts reflect a pooled judgment about the probabilities of events covered by the market. For example, people might buy contracts on which team (*A* or *B*, say), will win a World Cup soccer match. Initially, a market maker and a contract purchaser have to agree on a price for the contract. Suppose the agreed-upon price is $0.75 for a contract on team *A*. That is, the contract purchaser pays $0.75 for a $1.00 contract on team *A*. Then, if team *A* wins, the holder of the contract is paid $1.00 by the market maker. If team *A* doesn't win, the contract is worthless. Anytime before the game, however, people can buy and sell contracts to each other, and the price of the latest contract can be published for all to see—just like in a futures market for commodities such as corn or wheat. In this way, a price is established that reflects all of the information possessed by all of the people participating. This price will change over time as people take into account the latest information. If at some time the price for a $1.00 contract on team A is $0.80, for example, the subjective probability that team A will win can be taken at that time to be 0.8, and the odds in favor of team A would be 4 to 1.

Even when the outcome might be far in the future, or if there is no definite outcome, one can still use markets to establish probabilities. Market prices would fluctuate as new information comes in, and holders of contracts could always sell them to people who think they can make a profit by buying a contract now and selling it to someone else at a higher price later. And, someone who thinks the price will drop can sell short.

When experts participate in these markets, the probabilities ought eventually to be based on the opinions of the experts. As long as enough experts judge the probabilities to be different from those so far established by the market, and have confidence in their opinions as well, they can bid heavily with a view to making a large profit at the expense of the less well-informed participants. Their bidding will work to bring the probabilities more in accord with expert opinion.

These kinds of markets aren't just theoretical ideas. There actually are such markets. One, used primarily for teaching and research, is the Iowa Electronic Markets (IEM). Others are the Foresight Exchange (FX) and the Hollywood Stock Exchange (HSX).[3] Traders in these markets can "invest" in the outcomes of a wide variety of unresolved outcomes. For example, at FX, one can bet on whether a power plant will sell energy produced by nuclear fusion by December 31, 2045. (The probability of that was just below 85 percent in mid-2013.) At HSX, one can bet on who will win Oscar, Emmy, and Grammy awards. Prices in the latter market are said to correlate well with actual award outcome frequencies.

Although he probably didn't anticipate these sorts of markets, Justice Oliver Wendell Holmes, Jr. once wrote, "The best test of truth is the power of the thought to get itself accepted in the competition of the market."[4] I include this quote not because I endorse the idea that the best beliefs are those held by a majority of people. The crowd is often misled, especially the not-sufficiently informed crowd. On the other hand, I do think that the beliefs of experts, when unanimous or nearly so, are worth adopting as one's own—so long as one continues to monitor possible shifts in expert opinion.

Recall that in chapter 4, figure 2, I displayed some of the beliefs about global warming in a network. Statisticians and computer scientists call networks of this kind

"Bayesian belief networks." They have been used to represent and reason about knowledge in many different subject areas, including medicine, genomics, meteorology, and engineering. In some applications the networks are very large, often containing several hundreds or thousands of propositions.

The structure of a belief network encodes information about which beliefs directly affect other beliefs. To over-simplify, beliefs are influenced mainly by neighboring beliefs in the network. This structure, along with some additional data encoding how much a belief influences its network neighbors, can be used to compute the probabilities of beliefs given those of others. The mathematics of the probability computations are rather complex, so I won't go into them here. Instead, I'll use the global-warming network, repeated below in figure 3, to illustrate the main ideas.

Suppose first that increased levels of CO_2 in the atmosphere are actually observed and measured. Meteorologists can use those observations, together with known models about how atmospheric CO_2 causes heat retention, to estimate the probability that the atmosphere is retaining more heat. In turn, because atmospheric heat retention is a cause of global warming, meteorologists can use their computer models of this process to calculate the probability that the earth is indeed warming. This kind of reasoning, proceeding upward in the network, is called "causality reasoning," based as it is on causal models of physical processes.

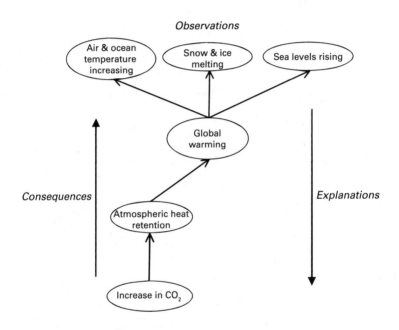

Figure 3 A Bayesian belief network

The structure of a belief network encodes information about which beliefs directly affect other beliefs. To over-simplify, beliefs are influenced mainly by neighboring beliefs in the network.

Next, going to the top of the network, suppose that sea levels are in fact rising as indicated by actual measurements. Can we work our way downward in the network to calculate how these observations affect the probability of global warming? We could use a causal model of how global warming affects the probability of rising sea levels. But that's reasoning in the opposite direction from what is desired here. What we want is the probability of global warming given that sea levels are rising. Reversing the direction of "probability flow" can be done by using a rule invented by an English clergyman, the Reverend Thomas Bayes, in the mid-1700s. What has come to be known as "Bayes' Rule" is used to reason "downward" in belief networks from effects to causes. That style of reasoning is called "evidential reasoning"—reasoning from evidence to possible causes. (It is also called "abductive reasoning.") It is what physicians do, albeit informally, when they use observed symptoms to infer probabilities of underlying causes of those symptoms.

Additionally, if we next learn that the temperatures of the air and ocean are rising, we can use another bout of evidential reasoning to increase further the probability that the earth is warming. Evidential reasoning can accumulate. Two or more pieces of *independent* evidence give extra support for a belief. To continue this example of how probabilities of propositions change based on evidence (or lack thereof), suppose at this stage that no measurements have yet been made about melting snow and ice. But, because that is a consequence of global warming (itself now estimated to be rather probable), we can use causality reasoning to estimate the probability of observing melting snow and ice. If we were to look and fail to observe melting snow and ice (contrary to what was predicted), that failure would, by evidential reasoning, reduce the probability of global warming. In fact though, as mentioned in chapter 4, snow and ice are actually observed to be melting, so the probability of global warming is increased rather than suffering a decrease.

In chapter 4, I mentioned another type of reasoning, namely "explaining away." If, for example, another highly probable cause could be found for global warming, such as an increase in heat energy coming from the sun, that cause would, by itself, reduce the probability that the underlying cause for global warming is atmospheric heat retention. Actually, no such alternative cause has yet been found to be very probable, so heat retention is not explained away. The actual numerical calculations used to assign probabilities to propositions in belief networks are very complex, but even for rather large networks computers can perform the necessary computations.

In their everyday reasoning activities, people frequently use informal versions of causality, evidential, and explaining-away methods. It is easy to be misled, however, by failing to appreciate some of the subtleties of probabilistic reasoning. Consider, for example, the theory that

In their everyday reasoning activities, people frequently use informal versions of causality, evidential, and explaining-away methods. It is easy to be misled, however, by failing to appreciate some of the subtleties of probabilistic reasoning.

dreams can forecast future events. You may have a dream that a friend died in a car crash and wake up the next morning to find out that your friend did indeed have a car accident. But one such incident like that hardly confirms the theory. You must consider a statistically adequate sample of dreams, in which hundreds (or maybe thousands) of them have no bearing at all on future events. It's more parsimonious to believe that the friend's car accident was just a random coincidence.

As another example, suppose someone tells you that a certain stock-market analyst, say, Mr. Smith, accurately predicted that the stock market would crash in October 1987. Before adopting the belief that Smith has unusually accurate prediction abilities and relying on his future forecasts, you would need to consider how he had done in the past, and to realize that of the various stock-market predictions by the many hundreds (perhaps thousands) of analysts it is likely that at least one of them (this time it was Smith) would have been right about October 1987. If you have enough forecasters, *someone* among them is bound to have been right about the past. Would Mr. Smith be right the next time? Well, maybe, if there really were some basis on which accurate predictions could be made. But, otherwise, success is just a chance event. As they say in investment circles, "past performance is no guarantee of future results."

REALITY AND TRUTH

Our beliefs are descriptions of *reality*. Some of them we even claim to be *true*. What can be said about the subjects of reality and truth? Let's discuss the subject of reality first. I believe that reality exists independently of our own thoughts and perceptions about it. The impact of reality on our senses (both natural and augmented senses) leads us to invent the concepts of various objects, properties, and relations, which we use in sentences to describe reality. One such sentence, for example, might be, "The San Andreas fault is a boundary between the Pacific and North American plates." That sentence is one of my beliefs—part of my *model* of reality. Faults, boundaries, and plates are examples of invented objects, which we use in a model of reality. I don't believe we should think of them as part of reality itself.

There are different philosophical points of view about reality. For example, one version of a doctrine called "realism" holds "that the objects the world contains exist independently of our thoughts about them or our perceptions of them."[1] Philosophers call the people who adopt this point of view "realists." I am not a realist because I think "objects" are concepts that we have invented, not "things" that actually exist in the world. To claim that objects actually *exist* in the world is to confuse our models of reality with reality itself. Using our model-building apparatus and informed by our perceptions, we can only say things *about* reality. We can never say what it *is*. And, most importantly, what we say about it is always subject to revision.

Several thinkers agree with this point of view, expressing it in various ways:

"Objects" do not exist independently of conceptual schemes. *We* cut up the world into objects when we introduce one or another scheme of description.

—Hilary Putnam, philospher[2]

There was no way to hook up ideas with things ... because ideas—mental representations—do not refer to things; they refer to other mental representations.

—Louis Menand, author, referring to thoughts of philosopher C. S. Peirce[3]

There is no quantum world. There is only an abstract physical description. It is wrong to think that the task of physics is to find out how nature *is*. Physics concerns what we can *say* about nature ...

—Niels Bohr, physicist[4]

The physicist *constructs* [my emphasis] what he terms the physical world, a concept which arises from a peculiar combination of certain observed facts and the reasoning provoked by their perception.

—Robert Lindsay and Henry Margenau, physicists[5]

Even some theologians around the time of Galileo agreed that there was a difference between reality itself and descriptions of reality. For example, they acknowledged that the heliocentric system of Galileo might be a useful *description* for calculating the predictions needed for navigation. Their argument with Galileo was not about which description was better, but about which of the systems, heliocentric or geocentric, was *real*. Of course, in my opinion, trying to decide what's *real* is a fool's errand. All we can do is create descriptions of reality—not decide what it *really is*. Galileo might have saved himself some trouble by claiming only that his description was the better one. But he undoubtedly thought it made sense to say that it was also *real*.

Turning now to the subject of truth, some philosophers claim that a true statement is one that "corresponds" with reality, that is, with the way things "actually are." That definition sounds seductively simple and obvious. However, I think the phrase "the way things actually are" is meaningless. Let's see why by examining how the correspondence theory is supposed to work. The sentence "Coal is black" is true, according to the correspondence theory of truth, if

Even some theologians around the time of Galileo agreed that there was a difference between reality itself and descriptions of reality.

coal (that object in the world referred to by the word "coal") actually is black (that property in the world referred to by the word "black"). What could be more obvious?

Indeed! But the problem is that what we think of as coal (that alleged object in the world) and blackness (that alleged property in the world) are *words* that denote concepts that we invent to help us carve up and describe reality. Objects and properties are components of our *models*, not of reality. As a slang expression would have it, "Reality doesn't know from coal"—it just *is*. Trying to describe how things actually are is a misguided attempt to say what reality *is*.

Other philosophers, recognizing some of the difficulties of the correspondence theory of truth, attempt to define truth using the idea of "coherence." In one version of the coherence theory of truth, each member of a set of beliefs can be considered true if, taken together, there are no contradictions among them, that is, if they are internally consistent. So, for example, the statements "all swans are white," and "Pollux is a black swan," do not cohere—they cannot both be true. But the statements "all swans are white," and "Castor is a white swan," do cohere—they could each be true. Short of having a way to evaluate the credibility of a set of statements in light of evidence, about all we can do is check to see if they are consistent. Someone confronted with a logical inconsistency among his or her beliefs should, at least, seek to adjust those beliefs to eliminate the inconsistency. The coherence theory of truth recalls Richard Rorty's statement, "Only a sentence can be relevant to the truth of another sentence."[6]

When members of a set of related beliefs have probability values associated with them, a generalized version of coherence involves checking to see if these probability values together satisfy the laws of probability theory. The methods for propagating probabilities among the various nodes in a Bayesian belief network ensure that the probabilities are mutually coherent.

One of the consequences of my view about truth and reality is that there are no "absolute truths" that are "out there" in some sense. When people say that such-and-such is *absolutely true*, I conclude that they believe "such-and-such" very, very strongly and that they don't think they will ever, ever change their minds about it. "Absolute truth" is just a label we apply to certain beliefs that are held very, very strongly and permanently. Some people have claimed that to say there are no absolute truths is self-contradictory because that statement itself is an absolute truth. But, I am not subject to that contradiction because I don't claim that my belief—that there are no absolute truths—is an absolute truth. It's just one of my strongly held beliefs.

What about mathematical and logical truths? Isn't it true (even absolutely true in some sense) that 2 + 2 = 4? Why quibble with that? Yes, there are mathematical and logical truths, but they depend on a specialized definition of truth used in mathematics and logic. There, truth has to do essentially with different ways of saying the same thing.

'Absolute truth' is just a label we apply to certain beliefs that are held very, very strongly and permanently.

For example, it is a mathematical truth that at least two of the sides of an isosceles triangle are equal. That fact is inherent in the definition of an isosceles triangle, namely that at least two of its angles are equal, plus some of the standard assumptions about plane geometry. Saying that the two sides of an isosceles triangle are equal doesn't say anything new beyond what was already implied by the definition and these assumptions. As a less mathematical example, if I already attach the label "true" to the belief "curing a cold takes seven days," I can also attach the label "true" to the belief "curing a cold takes a week." Nothing new there.

In responding to someone telling us that such-and-such is true, we might say "that's right," "that's accurate," or "that's correct," indicating that we also believe that such-and-such is true. Or we might say "that's wrong" if we don't believe it. There are lots of synonyms and antonyms for the word "true." In any case, upon learning about a belief of another person we have gained a new belief ourselves—a *meta-belief*, which is a belief about a belief. My belief that John believes (and does so strongly), that the earth is becoming warmer, for example, is a meta-belief. Would I say in this example that John "knows" that the earth is becoming warmer? Well, that really depends on how I want to use the word "know." If I believe strongly that the world is becoming warmer, then I might well say that, in addition to *my* knowing it, so does John. However, someone who doesn't believe that the world is becoming warmer might not want to say that John "knows" it because, he would ask, "how could someone 'know' something that I don't label as 'true'?" All such a person would be willing to say is that John believes it. Usage of these words is entirely up to the person using them, although it would help communication if we all agreed on definitions.

Not only is each of us able to use whatever words we choose in describing our own beliefs and the beliefs of others, but we are also able to believe what we want and with what strengths. We all are able to, and do, make our own different models of reality. The result is that some people are led to say such things as "that may be true for you, but it isn't true for me." Quite so! Such statements are related to a philosophical position called "relativism," which Richard Rorty has defined as "the view that every belief on a certain topic, or perhaps about any topic, is as good as every other."[7] Although everyone does have his or her own beliefs, I certainly don't believe (and would deny) that the beliefs of everyone are equally good.

How are we to judge, then, whether some beliefs are *better* than others? The answer is that we judge beliefs by comparing whatever predictions they might make with careful observations, and by seeking credible explanations for them and for the consequences of them. (This view is related to a doctrine called *instrumentalism* by philosophers.) The most disciplined way to make these judgments is part of the scientific method, which brings us to the subject of the next chapter.

THE SCIENTIFIC METHOD

The set of practices scientists use to tease out descriptions of reality has come to be called "the scientific method." As I have already mentioned, the scientific method is a highly disciplined, but still rather informal, application of the elements of critical thinking that many of us use quite naturally. In fact, Albert Einstein once said, "The whole of science is nothing more than a refinement of everyday thinking."[1] These refinements consist mainly of careful observations followed by creating and testing explanations for these observations. People as far back as the Babylonians and ancient Greeks used many of these strategies in their attempts to learn about the natural world.

Near the beginning of the eleventh century, al-Haytham, an Islamic scholar who lived in Basra and Cairo, wrote *The Book of Optics*, which included a theory of vision and a theory of light. According to one authority "Ibn al-Haytham was the pioneer of the modern scientific method.

With his book he changed the meaning of the term 'optics' and established experiments as the norm of proof in the field. His investigations are based not on abstract theories, but on experimental evidences, and his experiments were systematic and repeatable."[2] In particular, al-Haytham combined observations, experiments and rational arguments to support a theory of vision in which rays of light come from the objects seen rather than from the eyes that see them.

Notable European contributors to the development of the scientific method include Robert Grosseteste (c. 1175–1253), Roger Bacon (c. 1214–1294), Galileo (1564–1642), Francis Bacon (1561–1626), and René Descartes (1596–1650)—all preceding one of the greatest scientists of all time, Isaac Newton (1643–1727).

Today, the scientific method is employed throughout the world, having created an explosion of knowledge during the last few centuries. To be sure, the ways the method is applied in the laboratories of chemists, in the field work of geologists, in the observatories of astronomers, and at the desks of theorists are slightly different, but the spirit is the same: observe, explain, and test. In this chapter, I'll first describe what I think scientific knowledge itself is all about and then turn to the essential processes of science.

Scientific knowledge consists of many facts and theories—about objects, processes, and the relationships among them. Objects range from the billions of immense galaxies to the smallest sub-atomic particles. In between, there are stars and planets, life forms and their constituent components, chemical compounds, and atoms. Processes involving these objects include the Big Bang that started it all, the births and deaths of stars, the movements of continents, the changes in climate and weather, the evolution and behavior of all living things, the languages and migrations of peoples, the workings of the cell, the shuffling of DNA, and the behavior of subatomic particles, to name just a few that scientists identify and study. I remind the reader of Niels Bohr's statement in chapter 6 that these objects and processes are only abstract physical descriptions, and not to be thought of as how nature *is*. It takes many theories to describe the world scientifically, and so far no single one does the entire job. Instead, scientific knowledge consists of many, many theories, at many levels of detail and credibility, scattered around the world in books, journal articles, computer databases, and people's heads.

Some scientific knowledge can be called "textbook knowledge"—sufficiently regarded by the experts that it is taught to generations of new scientists. Much of quantum mechanics, for example, is now textbook knowledge. Some scientific knowledge, on the other hand, is "frontier knowledge," recently minted and still in need of testing. Ideas about the possible genetic causes of some diseases are examples of frontier knowledge. Whether in textbooks or at the frontier, *all* scientific knowledge is subject to change as scientists continue to observe, theorize, and test. New experiments with new observational equipment might require replacing existing knowledge with new knowledge. Yet, regardless of its tentative status, today's scientific knowledge constitutes the best descriptions of reality presently available.

Scientists distinguish between two main types of scientific knowledge, "facts" and "theories." Facts usually refer to the specific results of careful observations or experiments. For example, a scientist might say that it's a *fact* that a 10-kilogram object dropped from a height of 10 meters reached a velocity of 14 meters per second when it hit the ground. But he might also mention Galileo's *theory* that two heavy objects of different masses dropped simultaneously from the same height would reach the ground at the same time.

Theories are constructs meant to predict the results of observations or to explain in more detail already existing theories. For example, Newton's theories of motion and gravity constitute an explanation for planetary orbits (and much else). Theories can only be constructed out of concepts that are available at the time. Newton had available the concepts of distance, force, mass, orbits, and acceleration, and these were all that were needed to develop his theories of motion and gravity. Modern scientists, peering at the world with sensory augmentations—such as telescopes, microscopes, MRI machines, x-ray detectors, particle accelerators, and ultrasound machines—have invented newer concepts such as quasars, bacteria, dark energy, and quarks to describe what they see. These are all building blocks for explanatory theories.

Theories are usually represented by a combination of words and mathematical equations. Increasingly, they are also encoded as computer simulations. For example, there are simulations of the behavior of high temperature gasses, which embody relevant thermodynamic theory. These can be used to predict the behavior of gasses under many different conditions. Outcomes of the simulation can then be checked against actual measurements.

An acceptable theory must not only be consistent with any observations already made but must also be capable of predicting the results of new observations. That is, besides covering existing facts, a scientific theory must also extend its reach beyond those facts to predict how new observations might turn out. If these new predictions, when tested by careful experiments, are satisfied, the theory gains credibility. Otherwise, the theory loses credibility and either has to be revised or abandoned.

Scientific theories must satisfy other requirements also. For one, they have to be testable, and it has to be the case that they *might* fail the test. That is, all scientific theories must be *falsifiable*. So, even though a scientist might *hope* that her theory will be consistent with the results of future experiments designed to test it, it must at least be *conceivable* that it wouldn't be. Even though scientific theories must be falsifiable, saying that something is a theory (instead of a fact) does not necessarily cast doubt on it. Most textbook theories, for example, are highly credible—so credible that we label them "true" just like we label facts "true." Even so, we would never assign 100 percent probability to a theory, because then (according to a technical result in probability theory) it could never be weakened—whatever the evidence. In science, we are always willing to entertain the idea that a theory might be overturned.

To understand the importance of falsifiability, think of the game "twenty questions." You ask a series of yes-no questions trying to pin down what object someone is thinking about. You try to ask a question whose answer would provide you the most information. You never ask a question that you know ahead of time could only be answered "yes" because it wouldn't give you any new information at all about what the object might be. An experiment used to test a scientific theory is a question asked about reality. It attempts to divide the set of possible realities in two. A "yes" answer to the question says that reality must lie among one of the subsets; a "no" answer says reality must lie in the other subset. Because unfalsifiable theories can produce only "yes" answers, they don't tell us anything about reality. They aren't of any interest scientifically because the task of science is to say *something* about reality.

The most common kinds of unfalsifiable theories are those with an inexhaustible supply of free parameters—

"knobs" on the theory that can be adjusted as needed to be consistent with any new data. For example, theories about extrasensory perception (ESP) are especially prone to the "too-many-knobs" problem. ESP experimenters who devise tests for whether people can "read" a remote person's thoughts can usually think of excuses for never accepting a "no" answer. Any one of a potentially limitless number of parameters about the "state" of either the subject or of the remote person can be used to explain away a failure. One of them was having a "bad day." Or one of them was "trying too hard." Or, maybe it was the experimenter's fault. He was "too skeptical," and his "negative aura" interfered with the effect. Other free parameters may pertain to the kind of message that was supposed to be sent from sender to receiver. If an ESP experiment doesn't work, an ESP advocate might say that the subject matter was not "of the right type." Because there could be an infinite number of such excuses for failure, there is no possibility whatsoever of getting an answer that a committed ESP theorist would accept as "no." Such an infinitely expandable theory could never be inconsistent with any experimental test, so the theory doesn't really say anything about reality.

People have a lot of beliefs that are not falsifiable, and therefore such beliefs cannot be considered to be scientific. For example, most theories about immortality— that is, life after death in some form or other—cannot be tested, so they are not scientific theories, even though many people might believe them. Personally, I wouldn't recommend basing actions on them.

Karl Popper claimed that science advances mainly by falsifying old theories and replacing them with new ones that are immune to the particular failures of the old ones.[3] The new ones must be falsifiable also, but with different tests. No *scientific* theory can be immune from eventual falsification.

A desirable feature of scientific theories is that they be consistent with each other. However, many of today's theories, even textbook ones, are not. For example, Newton's gravitational theory, quantum mechanics, and Einstein's general theory of relativity are inconsistent with each other. But each is useful in its limited setting. Newton's theory describes the force of gravity between objects of rather large sizes and distances, quantum mechanics describes phenomena at the subatomic level, and Einstein's theory describes phenomena around really massive objects, like stars, and phenomena near the speed of light. Scientists and engineers use Newton's theory for calculating spacecraft trajectories and the orbits of planets, they use quantum mechanics for calculating the behavior of subatomic particles, and they use Einstein's theory for calculating how a massive star refracts light from a more distant star. (Actually, calculating the precise orbit of Mercury requires a relativistic correction because of its proximity to a massive body, the sun.)

People have a lot of beliefs that are not falsifiable, and therefore such beliefs cannot be considered to be scientific.

Physicists are still looking for a single theory—a "theory of everything"—that would unify electromagnetism, the strong and weak nuclear forces, quantum mechanics, and gravity. One candidate, string theory, proposes that all of the elementary particles—electrons, quarks, and so on—are tiny, tiny strings, vibrating in ten (or, in some versions, eleven) dimensions.[4] Six of these dimensions are rolled up into such small formats that we—so far—experience only the other four dimensions of space-time. String theory is still very much frontier science, and many scientists think that it's not really a scientific theory because it's unfalsifiable. There are no known experiments that could test it. But, who knows? Maybe someone will come up someday with a test.

For the moment we must be satisfied with specialized theories having different domains of applicability within which each makes accurate and useful predictions. One just has to be careful to use the theories appropriate to their settings—settings in which their inconsistencies with other theories aren't evident.

Scientific knowledge is produced by a highly interdependent and rather messy social medley of observations, theorizing, experimental tests, and yet more theorizing and tests—all occurring in a maelstrom of criticism, debate, and wild speculations. If one looks at the history of science, the whole process seems more like the opportunistic communal solving of several jigsaw puzzles, with many participants and vocal kibitzers, than it does a well-ordered, systematic effort to describe the natural world. Scientific discovery is strewn with examples in which scientists behave more like wandering sleepwalkers than like wide-awake explorers.[5] The biologist François Jacob described one of his breakthroughs as the result of "night science," which he defined as "a stumbling, wandering exploration of the natural world that relies on intuition as much as it does on the cold, orderly logic of 'day science.'"[6]

One shouldn't, therefore, understand the phrase "the scientific method" to be anything like a simple crank-turning process for producing scientific knowledge. Scientists are human beings with the usual prejudices, egos, fears of failure, hopes for success, and all the other hindrances to objectivity. Nevertheless, science has given us, over the centuries, descriptions of reality sufficiently attuned to its workings that we are able to cure and prevent many diseases, send spacecraft to the edge of our solar system, build nano-devices, provide standards of living way beyond those of the richest ancient kings, and (sadly) produce thermonuclear explosions. So, even though some have said that science is merely "one particular way of knowing, no better than any others," science, even with all of its missteps (and maybe because of some of them), has produced results that none of the others, whatever they might be, can come close to matching.

Not only is the scientific method used to test theories that describe present reality, but it can also be used to test theories about past reality. There are theories about the birth of the universe as a Big Bang, for example. One consequence of that cosmological theory is that stars and galaxies should all be receding from the earth (and from each other), and that consequence is consistent with modern astronomical observations. We can't do any staged experiments involving a repeat of the Big Bang, so passive observations must suffice. Much of science, such as geology and paleoanthropology, is concerned with past events—as is the subject of human history. We can evaluate theories about these past events by making predictions about what the theory claims we might find by subsequent "digging." (Some people call the predictions made from theories about past events "postdictions.")

How science actually progresses is what books and articles on the history of science are all about. For example, one fascinating part of that history is how our ideas about the nature of electromagnetic waves gradually developed over the last few centuries—progressing from early studies of the properties of light all the way up through quantum mechanics. An abbreviated description of part of that history will give a flavor of how scientific knowledge evolves, building as it does on chance discoveries and previous theories.

After Isaac Newton's work with optics in the mid-1600s, people experimented with prisms to refract light into its constituent colors, which were projected as bands on a screen. In 1800, William Herschel, a British astronomer, observed that "something" was making a thermometer hotter when it was placed near the "un-illuminated" part of the screen next to the band of red light. Herschel theorized that there must be some "invisible" light coming through the prism impinging on the band below red (later called "infrared"). A year later, the German physicist Johann Wilhelm Ritter thought that perhaps an opposite, or cooling, effect might occur just beyond the band of violet light. One of his experiments found something else, namely that "something" just beyond the violet band darkened paper soaked with silver chloride. Here was yet more invisible light, later called "ultraviolet." Experiments showed that both types of these newly discovered light "rays" traveled in straight lines, exactly like visible light.

In another "territory" of science in the late 1700s and early 1800s, people such as Benjamin Franklin and Alessandro Volta were observing electrical activity of various sorts and constructing theories about it. Electricity's twin, magnetism, was known from ancient times. A connection between these two previously separate phenomena was first observed by Hans Christian Ørsted (a Danish physicist and chemist) in 1820. He was preparing materials for a lecture when he accidentally noticed that a compass needle moved when he switched a nearby current on and off. Immediately thereafter, André-Marie Ampère (a French physicist and mathematician) developed a mathematical theory to represent the magnetic forces between current-carrying conductors. Thus, the idea of "electromagnetism" was born.

In the 1830s, the English chemist and physicist Michael Faraday developed the concept of an "electromagnetic force field." Building on that idea, in the 1860s James Clerk Maxwell, a Scottish physicist and mathematician, produced a mathematical theory of these fields and their propagation as waves. He showed that one consequence of the equations constituting his theory was that the speed of electromagnetic waves was approximately the same as the already-measured speed of light. This coincidence led him to claim that light itself was also an electromagnetic wave.[7]

Soon after Maxwell's work, various physicists and engineers, primarily in Germany, were experimenting with partially evacuated glass enclosures called Crookes tubes. When the cathode and anode elements in such a tube were connected to an electrical source, a bluish fluorescent glow appeared to project to the end of the tube. Specially designed experiments revealed that the glow at the end of the tube surrounded a sharp-edged shadow cast by the tube's anode. In 1869, Johann Hittorf concluded that something must be traveling in straight lines from the cathode (toward the anode) to cast the shadow, and in 1876, Eugen Goldstein proved that these "somethings" came from the cathode, and named them cathode rays

(*Kathodenstrahlen*).[8] There was debate at the time about whether these rays were tiny particles or electromagnetic radiation. In 1896, the English physicist J. J. Thompson and others showed that the rays consisted of previously unknown negatively charged particles—now called electrons—and that they had a mass approximately equal to about a thousandth of the mass of the hydrogen atom. Therefore, the Crookes tube cathode rays, being particles, were not themselves electromagnetic waves.

In the mid-1890s, however, the German physicist Wilhelm Röntgen showed that when these particles struck the anode or glass enclosure of a Crookes tube, they produced yet a new kind of radiation that could travel through various materials outside of the tube. He called them "x-rays" to indicate that they were an unknown type of radiation. In one of his experiments, he used them to photograph his wife's hand—the first x-ray of a human body part. Later experiments showed that the paths of x-rays were bent in crystals in the same way that the paths of light were bent in optical gratings, providing evidence that x-rays were another kind of electromagnetic radiation.

Meanwhile, people were curious about the space-permeating medium, the so-called luminiferous aether, thought to be required for the propagation of electromagnetic waves. Was it like the air through which sound waves propagated? The speed of the earth around the sun had already been measured, but what about the speed of the earth through this aether? Equivalently, what was the speed of the aether "wind" as it brushed by the earth? Two American scientists, Albert Michelson and Edward Morley, conceived an experiment to measure the speed of this wind. It involved measuring the difference in the speed of light traveling in two different directions relative to the motion of the earth. Their experiments, performed in 1887, showed no difference beyond possible measurement error. Two important conclusions followed from their results: first, the speed of light, denoted by c, was constant regardless of its direction relative to the earth, and second, the imagined aether wind had no speed at all. So, if there was no wind, there was not any such aether.

Of course, Michelson and Morley were disappointed with their negative result. They were never quite convinced of the nonexistence of the aether and looked for flaws or errors in their experimental setup. (That's one of the ways scientists, being human and committed to their ideas, can deal with failed experiments.) Michelson also thought that perhaps the earth "dragged" the aether along with it; that would explain away the zero wind speed. Gradually though, amid much scientific discussion and with the negative results of additional experiments by Michelson and Morley and others, the theory about the existence of the aether had to be abandoned. Apparently, electromagnetic waves could travel through empty space without a medium.

The Dutch physicist Hendrik Lorentz was one of those who developed a theory for why the speed of light was constant regardless of direction. He proposed that moving bodies contract in the direction of motion. Any "ruler" used to measure the speeds of two light beams would contract precisely enough to yield equal speed values.

In 1905, motivated by Maxwell's theory of electromagnetism, Albert Einstein published his special theory of relativity. Among the theory's predictions was that the lengths of things would contract in their direction of motion. And, clocks would run more slowly in their direction of motion. These contraction effects are negligible at ordinary speeds but become dramatic at speeds approaching the speed of light. Both predictions have been confirmed by many subsequent experiments. Another consequence of special relativity is that mass and energy are equivalent ($E = mc^2$), which has been confirmed by particle accelerators and dramatized by nuclear explosions.

Theories about electromagnetic waves get even more interesting in the early years of the twentieth century. In 1905, using Max Planck's earlier hypothesis that energy levels can only be changed by discrete amounts or "quanta," Albert Einstein proposed that light (indeed, all electromagnetic radiation) consists of individual particles, later called "photons." The energy of these photons is proportional to the frequency of the radiation. Einstein's photon theory was a major step in what came to be called "quantum mechanics."

So what is the "real nature" of light—waves or particles? Well, it depends on what we try to do with light. Because models are constructions, people can only build models out of the mental materials at hand. The idea of a particle and the idea of a wave are both concepts that are grounded in the everyday physical experiences of people. Attempts to explain what happens when a beam of light passes through a narrow slit and produces bright and dim patterns on a screen naturally bring to mind how the crests and troughs of intersecting waves at the seashore strengthen and cancel each other. Attempts to explain how light exerts pressure to move a tiny metal surface naturally bring to mind a stream of particles impacting the surface. So far, we have no everyday experiences for building a single, consistent, intuitively understandable theory of light.

However, thanks to further developments in quantum mechanics by Niels Bohr, Arnold Sommerfeld, Erwin Schrödinger, Werner Heisenberg, Paul Dirac, and many others, both the particle-like and the wave-like behaviors of light can be explained by a single mathematical description. But, because intuitive models are so much more satisfying and compelling than ones built from mathematics alone, both the wave and particle models survive, and are useful, even though they are inconsistent. One just has to be careful to use the one appropriate to the circumstances.

Many of the ideas of quantum mechanics, such as "superposition" and "entanglement" still have no satisfying, intuitive explanations—yet they are described mathematically in ways that make consistently confirmed laboratory predictions. There are physicists who claim not to be bothered by this lack of a mental picture; they belong to what some call the "shut-up-and-calculate" school. So long as the model makes good predictions, who cares? Even though quantum mechanics is beyond the comprehension of most of us, it is vital to the development of much of modern technology. Examples include lasers, computer chips, electron microscopes and magnetic resonance imaging. In the future, we may even have quantum computers for performing certain tasks much, much faster than even our fastest current computers.

The entire process of filling in the jigsaw puzzles that led us from optical prisms to quantum mechanics was accompanied by the publication of peer-reviewed scientific papers, by attempts to repeat experiments, and by the criticisms of other scientists. Trustworthy scientific knowledge depends on these very important community efforts. Community participation begins with the peer-reviewed publication of a scientific result in an appropriate journal. Other scientists who are able to read and understand this result can then offer criticisms and, in the case of a new experimental result, can attempt to repeat the experiment.

Debate and criticism are extremely important to enhance objectivity in science. As the historians Joyce Appleby, Lynn Hunt, and Margaret Jacob put it:

> [Objectivity] does not simply reside within each individual, but rather is achieved by criticism, contention, and exchange. Without the social process of science—cumulative, contested, and hence at moments ideological—there is no science as it has come to be known since the seventeenth century. Criticism fosters objectivity and thereby enhances reasoned inquiry. Objectivity is not a stance arrived at by sheer willpower, nor is it the way most people, most of the time, make their daily inquiries. Instead it is the result of the clash of social interests, ideologies, and social conventions within the framework of object-oriented and disciplined knowledge-seeking.[9]

Though objectivity can be "fostered," it probably can never be completely achieved. As the chemist and philosopher Michael Polanyi put it: "complete objectivity ... is a delusion and is in fact a false ideal."[10] Nevertheless, scientists must try.

Scientists debate and challenge theory and experimental results in many ways. People who argue against a theory might claim that the experiment supporting the theory was flawed or that its results are erroneous. For example, people pointed out flaws in the cold-fusion experiments performed by Stanley Pons and Martin Fleischmann, and flaws are often found in experiments purporting to support ESP. To guard against flaws, it's important that critical experiments be done very carefully and repeated by *independent* investigators—scientists who have a different emotional stake in the outcome of their experiments. If flaws in the experiments supporting a theory cannot be found, opponents of the theory might be able to suggest a more credible alternative theory that better explains the experimental results. Or, they can claim that new experimental results are inconsistent with the theory.

People who argue in support of a theory can cite either the positive results of repeated experiments or of other confirmed new predictions. Or they can mention an agreed-upon underlying theory that supports the theory in question. To counter objections to a theory, proponents might cite evidence against competing theories. In case an experiment fails to confirm a theory, its proponents might try to explain away these negative results, as Michelson and Morley tried to do. In the history of scientific debate, which is often raucous but always necessary, it's easy to find all of these kinds of arguments.

There are some additional factors that affect the credibility of a theory and that provide rationale for debate and criticism. Among these are *parsimony*, *explanatory power*, and *boldness*. Usually the simplest theory consistent with all of the data is afforded higher credibility than more complex theories. This preference is called the "principle of parsimony" and is sometimes called the "Occam's razor principle." William of Occam was a fourteenth-century logician and Franciscan friar alleged to have said something like, "Entities should not be multiplied unnecessarily." The "razor" is used to shave away the unnecessary entities of the more complex theory.

To some extent, simplicity is in the eye of the beholder and depends on the language being used to describe theories, but there are some useful measures. One such is the number of entities required by the theory. For example, in the Ptolemaic theory, which was *the* dominant theory in the European Middle Ages, the sun, moon, and planets revolved in circles around the fixed, central earth. The radii of these circles were entities required by the theory. But to make the theory consistent with astronomical observations, the planets had to do little dances in small circles superimposed on their large circular orbits. These small circles were called "epicycles," additional entities needed to preserve the earth-centric theory. The heliocentric theory (a theory proposed as early as the third century BCE by Aristarchus of Samos) was revived by Copernicus and was later modified by Kepler to be consistent with data gathered by Tycho Brahe. It had the planets all going around the sun in elliptical orbits. Each orbit could be described by just two entities, namely the spatial locations of the two foci. The competing Ptolemaic theory could be—and was—adjusted so that it also matched Brahe's data. The adjustment consisted of adding epicycles to the epicycles—yet more entities. Though both theories were consistent with the data, the Keplerian theory, with its fewer entities, was the more parsimonious and therefore prevailed.

There is no reason to believe that reality itself is simple (and thus might best be described by simple theories), but there is a valid technical reason to prefer simpler theories as better descriptions of reality. It's because each of the entities in a theory is like a knob that can be adjusted as needed to make a theory consistent with the experimental data. The more knobs there are to twiddle, the more different specific theories there are to select from. And the more theories there are to select from, the more likely it is that one would be selected that wouldn't be very good at making new predictions—even though it did happen to fit the data at hand. All that the extra knobs can do is capture idiosyncrasies in the data rather than any underlying regularities of reality. Statisticians, for example, have long known that a simple model that fits the data is more likely than a complex model to make good predictions.[11]

The *explanatory power* of a theory also contributes to its credibility. Theories that explain independent observations in several separate subject areas are said to have great explanatory power. For example, in addition to sea levels rising, air and ocean temperatures rising, and glaciers melting, there are many more independent sources of evidence supporting the theory of climate change. Seasonal migrations of animals are happening earlier in spring and later in autumn, plants are flowering earlier and going dormant later, and extreme weather phenomena (such as hurricanes and floods) are becoming more prevalent. Global warming has impressive explanatory power.

I could cite several other examples of theories with great explanatory power. Plate tectonics is strongly supported by observations in a number of disparate fields including geology, biology, paleontology, seismology, geography, volcanology, and geophysics. Evolution explains a whole sweep of observations about living things—their diversity, relatedness, and behaviors, and even such minutia as why some of them have vestigial organs and appendages.

If theories in different areas can be regarded as special cases of a more general theory, then the more general theory has—in the words of the biologist Edward O. Wilson—the property of *consilience*. Consilient theories cover broad areas and thus are accorded high credibility. For example, Newton's theory of gravitation linked heaven and earth—explaining not only earth-bound falling bodies but planetary orbits as well. Newton seems to have been the first to propose that the laws governing earthbound objects also governed objects everywhere else—they were *universal*. And Maxwell's electrodynamics linked electricity, magnetism, radio waves and light waves—subsuming earlier theories of Ampère, Carl Friedrich Gauss, and Faraday.

Theories that make surprising, bold, and testable predictions—predictions that differ substantially from what our other theories and common sense might have told us—are especially noteworthy. Karl Popper defined a *bold theory* as "one that takes a great risk of being false— if matters could be otherwise, and seem at the time to be otherwise."[12] If these surprising predictions stand up to experiments, the theories are given higher rank than theories that make only very conservative predictions. Scientists insist, however, that unusually bold theories must pass unusually rigorous tests. Because bold theories run a "great risk of being false," it's not surprising that they often fail. It's only when they don't fail harsh tests that one accords them high credibility.

Einstein's theories of special and general relativity are examples of bold theories that made surprising predictions subsequently confirmed by careful experiments. Two particularly important predictions of general relativity are that a gravitational body, such as the earth, would warp space and time around it and that its rotation would pull space and time along with it. An extremely expensive and long-lasting experiment, called Gravity Probe B, confirmed both of these predictions by monitoring the orientations of ultrasensitive space-borne gyroscopes relative to a distant guide star.[13]

Another example of a bold theory is the theory of cold fusion by Stanley Pons and Martin Fleischmann. The theory was certainly bold because it challenged well-established nuclear theory and made surprising predictions that could be experimentally tested. But, so far, it has failed all of its tests.

A primary distinction between science and other attempts to describe and explain the world we live in is that science, when it lives up to its ideals, tolerates—indeed encourages—critical discussion. As the philosopher David Miller put it: "Every effort must be made to provide criticism in the fullest measure. Reality must be ransacked for refutations."[14]

Another benefit of criticism is that it helps control the population explosion generated by prolific theorists. People can cook up theories faster than they can be thoroughly evaluated. As Edward O. Wilson wrote, "Anyone can have a theory; pay your money and take your choice among the theories that compete for your attention. Voodoo priests sacrificing chickens to please spirits of the dead are working with a theory. So are millenarian cultists watching the Idaho skies for signs of the Second Coming."[15] Many theories are rejected simply because scientists think they would be a waste of their time.

Eventually, after debate has settled down, scientists usually reach a consensus about the credibility of a theory. Using words similar to those suggested by Wilson, most scientists in a given discipline come to agree that a theory in their discipline is either "suggestive," "persuasive," "compelling," or "obvious."[16] And, these appellations can change as a scientific field matures.

Even after a consensus about a theory has been reached, however, new experiments and observations might create unresolvable problems for the theory—problems that cannot be solved by minor patches. In such cases, the old theory might eventually be replaced by a brand new and radically different one. The historian of science, Thomas Kuhn, has called such abrupt theory changes, "paradigm shifts."[17] In a paradigm shift, the old theory is rejected in favor of a new one, or maybe it is just put on a shelf for occasional use under special circumstances. I have already talked about one series of increasingly better planetary theories—Ptolemaic, Keplerian, and Newtonian—all examples of paradigm shifts. The moves to relativity theory and to quantum mechanics are two more examples.

No discussion of the scientific method would be complete without mentioning the philosopher of science Paul Feyerabend's opinion that acquiring new and improved knowledge about the natural world often depends on violating some of the practices of the scientific method. His excellent book, *Against Method*, gives several examples and argues for the importance of serendipity and historical and personal factors in scientific inquiry. He claims, for example: "There is no idea, however ancient and absurd, that is not capable of improving our knowledge."[18] In the practice of science, inventing theories requires Feyerabend's "anything goes" attitude, and evaluating theories requires detailed and thorough criticism.

Although many aspects of the scientific method, such as performing complicated laboratory experiments, would not be applicable for evaluating our everyday beliefs, we can, with some effort, adopt some of the practices that scientists routinely employ. For example, we can check the consequences of a belief. Are *they* believable? If one of our beliefs contradicts another, we can try to resolve the conflict by adjusting one or both of them. We can ask if a belief has a believable explanation. If the belief is itself an explanation for other beliefs or for observations, is it the simplest explanation? If a belief touches on a subject about which there is expert and agreed-upon opinion, we can compare our belief with that opinion. And, we can discuss our beliefs with others who may have different beliefs. Ideas that are immune from debate can never be in good standing in science, nor should they be in daily life.

Ideas that are immune from debate can never be in good standing in science, nor should they be in daily life.

ROBOT BELIEFS

Like humans, many robots and other computer systems are capable of complex behaviors, both physical and cognitive. On the physical side, for example, Google is developing automobiles that can drive themselves completely autonomously. According to a Google blog:[1]

> Our automated cars, manned by trained operators, just drove from our Mountain View campus to our Santa Monica office and on to Hollywood Boulevard. They've driven down Lombard Street [which is very steep and curvy], crossed the Golden Gate bridge, navigated the Pacific Coast Highway, and even made it all the way around Lake Tahoe. All in all, our self-driving cars have logged over 140,000 miles [with only two human interventions].

In addition to their TV camera visual systems, GPS, and lidar sensors, Google's self-driving automobiles have access to maps, data from Google's Street View and vehicle driving codes, along with various other sources of knowledge needed for legal and competent driving behavior.

On the cognitive side, the IBM computer, Watson defeated two human champions in the quiz show game *Jeopardy!* televised in February 2011. Watson had access to four terabytes of data, including millions of documents, dictionaries, encyclopedias, and other reference materials.

We certainly would say that human automobile drivers have beliefs about driving and that human *Jeopardy!* contestants have beliefs about literature, culture, sports, and other subjects. Couldn't we say then that Google's self-driving automobiles and IBM's Watson have beliefs, too?

We ascribe beliefs (along with other mental qualities) to humans because, as the philosopher Daniel Dennett argues, doing so helps us explain and predict their behavior.[2] The same holds, he claims, for objects like robots and computer systems. In ordinary conversation, we often attribute knowledge and beliefs to computer systems. It's common to say things like "the word-processing program *believed* I wanted that lowercase *i* capitalized." Or "the chess-playing program *knew* it had me checkmated." It's more convenient to describe computational behavior that way than it would be, for example, to refer to the actual computer code that automatically capitalizes a typed isolated lowercase *i*. Even though psychologists and neuroscientists don't yet know very much about what exactly beliefs are or how they are represented in human brains, engineers know exactly how knowledge is represented in the robots and computer systems that they build. They get to decide whether or not to use the word "belief" as part of the technical vocabulary used to describe how these systems work.

The computer pioneer John McCarthy argued for ascribing beliefs to machines. For example, he claimed we could say a thermostat's "belief" that a room is too cold is what leads it to turn on the furnace. As he put it, "When the thermostat believes the room is too cold or too hot, it sends a message saying so to the furnace."[3] Although in the case of a simple device like a thermostat, he admits, we wouldn't need to talk about its beliefs because its operation is so easily understood using a description involving a bi-metallic strip triggering an electrical switch.

For more complex systems though, such as computers, it's not only possible but also useful to provide a technical definition for belief. I would say that all of the information represented declaratively in a computer system's memory constitutes its beliefs. For example, Shakey, the Stanford Research Institute robot built in the 1960s, had a large database of declarative sentences, including ones like "Doorway 17 connects Room 32 with Hallway 4." (The actual form of those sentences used a computer-friendly language called the "first-order predicate calculus" rather than English.) Shakey used "beliefs" such as these to help it decide how to navigate from room to room.

The most common type of database system represents its data declaratively in what is called a "relational" format. We could say, for example, that a program, such as Microsoft's Outlook, believes "John Jones's home address is 1342 Elm Street" if it contained the computer equivalent of that sentence in its database. One could even say that it *knew* it if it represented it unequivocally, as Outlook does. It is common, for example, to say something like, "My computer *knows* the names, addresses, and phone numbers of many of my friends."

Because so much of their information is represented declaratively, we can say that Google's driverless cars had beliefs about driving and that Watson had beliefs about the many things needed to compete on *Jeopardy!*. Watson's beliefs, many of them in the form of actual English sentences, allowed it to conclude, for example, that Sir Christopher Wren designed Emmanuel and Pembroke Colleges. Watson believed that answer with a confidence value of 85 percent, as a snapshot from the telecast shows. (See figure 4.) It was confident enough to act on that belief by delivering that answer.

Many modern information systems organize their declarative knowledge in networks. The links and nodes of the network permit a compact representation of sentence-type information. Figure 5 is an example. The diagram is a way of representing sentences such as "Gio is a robot," "Mia is a human," and "Mia programmed Gio." It can

Figure 4 Watson's confidence values

also be used to derive additional facts such as "Mia is an agent." Such diagrams are called "semantic networks." (In computers, they are represented, of course, by computer code—not by pictures. The picture equivalent is easier for humans to understand than would be the computer code itself.) Because these networks express information about various entities and their properties, they are often called "ontologies," using a term borrowed from philosophy having to do with "things that exist." Ontologies are used to organize information in the World Wide Web, in software engineering, in biomedical informatics, in business enterprises, and in library science, among other applications. Some psychologists think that humans store their beliefs in mental structures that are somewhat like ontologies.

A computer system's beliefs can be updated by additions, modifications, or deletions of propositions in the system's database. Modifications can be made either by human programmers or, more interestingly, by the systems themselves as they interact with their environments and with data. Self-modification is an example of what artificial intelligence researchers call "machine learning." Some robots, such as Google's self-driving automobiles, continuously update their world models based on what their various sensors tell them about their environments.

There are also several computer systems that are able to extract logical propositions from the millions of Web pages that contain English sentences. These propositions

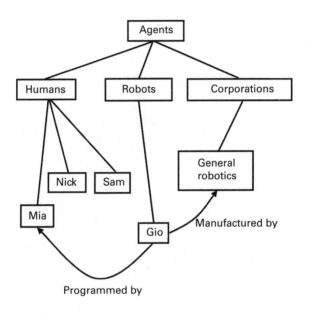

Figure 5 A semantic network

A computer system's beliefs can be updated by additions, modifications, or deletions of propositions in the system's database.

can then be added to a computer database of declarative knowledge that can be queried to obtain answers to questions posed by a human user.[4]

As another example, a traffic-prediction system called JamBayes,[5] a precursor to Microsoft's Clearflow system, uses a belief network of propositions automatically constructed from five years of traffic data and other information, including accidents and collisions, weather, major sporting games, and events in the region.

Robots are also able to learn procedural knowledge, such as control programs for performing specific tasks. Several approaches have been investigated. One is called "learning by demonstration," in which a human teacher demonstrates for a robot how to perform a complex task. The robot's sensory system observes several examples of how the task is performed. From this sensory information (generalized over many demonstrations), control programs are automatically synthesized and adjusted until the robot can perform the task on its own. In one example, a robot learns how to prepare orange juice.[6] As the article notes, this task might "involve multiple subtasks, such as juicing the orange, throwing the rest of the orange in the trash and pouring the liquid in a cup. Furthermore, each time this task is performed, the robot will need to contend with changes such as displacement of the items' locations." If failures occur, the human teacher simply has to provide more demonstrations.

Another approach involves what is called "reinforcement learning," in which a robot's control program is "rewarded" by making those actions that contribute to accomplishing some specific given task more likely to be taken in the future. After many trials, the robotic device will "learn" a program that performs the task. A full explanation of how the process works is rather complex, but the method has achieved some impressive results, such as having a model helicopter learn to perform aerobatic maneuvers.[7]

What do the beliefs of computers and robots have to do with human beliefs? Our various engineering devices have often served as inspirations for understanding biological phenomena. The heart is a kind of pump, the eye is a kind of lens and camera, the muscles and tendons in arms and legs are like cables pulling on levers, the ear is a kind of microphone, and the brain was once considered to be a kind of hydraulic apparatus, then a telephone switchboard, and now a computer. Considering how computer systems acquire, create, organize, and evaluate beliefs might provide a useful guide for how people do these things. Comparative studies often help illuminate the subjects being compared. For example, studying geologic processes on Mars and other planets leads to generalizations that give us a better understanding of the earth's geology. Studying different languages contributes to useful generalizations about linguistics. I think additional insight about human beliefs may be gained by comparing us to robots.

Considering how computer systems acquire, create, organize, and evaluate beliefs might provide a useful guide for how people do these things.

Like robots, I think that we humans are machines—albeit very, very complex ones, still barely understood. Regarding our ability to form useful beliefs, I think we are pretty much in the same boat as robots are. Just like robots, we use our perceptual apparatus to create models of our environment. Like robots, some of these models are in the form of declarative sentences, that is, beliefs. And, like the more advanced robots, we use reasoning abilities to derive consequences and propose explanations for our beliefs. Some robots are even able to test their beliefs by proposing and performing experiments. Robots do not have any "magical," nonphysical methods for obtaining information. I don't believe humans do either.

BELIEF TRAPS

I have stressed throughout this book that our beliefs should be subject to change. Scientists are used to having their theories replaced by better ones. Why shouldn't we regard our everyday beliefs as tentative also? Even if we don't replace a belief with a brand new one, we should be willing at least to change the strength of a belief based on new information and after discussions with others.

While we may be intellectually willing to accept *in principle* that our beliefs should be tentative, it can be very difficult actually to change beliefs. It's easy to get trapped with beliefs that wouldn't survive critical evaluation. There are several psychological reasons for these "belief traps" as well as reasons that have to do with lifestyle. Let's look first at the obstacles to belief change caused by one's lifestyle and attitudes.

Some people don't get around much. They don't read material that challenges their beliefs, and they don't participate in discussions with people who hold beliefs different from their own. The result of living that kind of a life can be belief stagnation. Actually, the result can be even worse. A book by Cass R. Sunstein, a law professor at Harvard, mentions studies showing that when people discuss beliefs only with like-minded people, their beliefs become more extreme.[1] For example, "When like-minded liberals discuss climate change, they end up more alarmed about climate change. When conservatives gather to discuss same-sex unions, they oppose them even more."[2]

Whether we are open to discussions with others or not, technology is beginning to force a certain amount of intellectual isolation on all of us. In his book, *The Filter Bubble*, Eli Pariser claims that as we interact more-and-more with sites like Google and Facebook, we are increasingly presented mainly with information filtered to match our own preexisting views and preferences.[3] Those sites, whose goals are to present us with information (and advertisements) fashioned especially to our own individual tastes, tend to isolate us in a bubble of like-minded views—a bubble that filters out discordant information.

Other obstacles to belief change are psychological—built into our mechanisms for processing information. For example, the psychologist Daniel T. Gilbert describes two separate mental activities for processing a new piece of information, namely *comprehension* and *assessment*.[4] Comprehension involves understanding a proposition or

When people discuss beliefs only with like-minded people, their beliefs become more extreme.

group of propositions that we hear or read. Assessment involves comparing what is comprehended with other information. Most importantly, we comprehend first and assess later! Gilbert and many others claim that we are automatically disposed to believe what we comprehend *before* assessment has a chance to operate. The process of assessment, however, takes more mental effort than the automatic process of comprehension. As Gilbert puts it, when people are "faced with shortages of time, energy, or conclusive evidence, [they] fail to unaccept the ideas that they involuntarily accept during comprehension." He goes on to conclude that "findings from a multitude of research literatures converge on a single point: People are credulous creatures who find it very easy to believe and very difficult to doubt."

Yet, doubt is a valuable defense against belief traps. As the physicist Richard Feynman said:[5]

> I can live with doubt and uncertainty and not knowing—I think it's much more interesting to live not knowing than to have answers that might be wrong. I have approximate answers and possible beliefs and different degrees of certainty about different things but I'm not absolutely sure of anything and there are many things I don't know anything about.

What about the assessment process itself? There are psychological processes at work there, too. *Confirmation bias* and *disconfirmation bias* both interfere with impartial belief assessment. Confirmation bias is a tendency to favor information that supports an already-held belief. Disconfirmation bias is a tendency to disregard or ignore information that is contrary to an already-held belief. These biases have their greatest influence for those beliefs that are strongly held or that have been held for a long time.

These biases work against changing one's mind, even in situations in which both sides of a contentious issue are presented. In fact, after hearing evidence pro and con on an issue, people tend to become even more extreme in their views. Sunstein's book cites several academic studies in which groups of people holding different views about some proposition or issue are presented with arguments on both sides. Instead of people's beliefs being softened, the beliefs of the two groups get even farther apart. Summarizing the reasons in a *New York Times* article, Sunstein says:[6]

> When people get information that supports what they initially thought, they give it considerable weight. When they get information that undermines their initial beliefs, they tend to dismiss it.
>
> In this light, it is understandable that when people begin with opposing initial beliefs on, say, the

death penalty, balanced information can heighten their initial disagreement. Those who tend to favor capital punishment credit the information that supports their original view and dismiss the opposing information. The same happens on the other side. As a result, divisions widen.

Why do we have these confirmation and disconfirmation biases? Are they built in to the way we process information? As one observer puts it, "Accuracy of belief isn't our only cognitive goal. Our other goal is to validate our pre-existing beliefs, beliefs that we've been building block by block into a cohesive whole our entire lives." Our beliefs are like a fortress that must be protected, and our brains seem wired to do that.[7]

To counter these biases, one might look to see what the experts believe. It would seem foolhardy to believe something whose strength is based on confirmation and disconfirmation biases when experts believe the opposite. Of course, especially in frontier science, one should always view expert opinion with caution. But even then, it would seem wiser to live with beliefs having only middling credibility than to assign high strength to beliefs about very controversial subjects.

What about our vaunted reasoning processes? Can't they be used to counter psychological obstacles to evaluating beliefs? Reasoning, properly used, can certainly reveal beliefs that conflict with our other beliefs. And being aware of these conflicts can lead us to change beliefs to resolve inconsistencies. But if our reasoning processes are guided more by our emotions than by logic, we can be led astray. Brain researchers have even used neuro-imaging techniques to identify specific regions in our brains thought to be responsible for non-logical reasoning, a kind they call "motivated reasoning." These regions, they claim, work to converge "on judgments that minimize negative and maximize positive affect states associated with threat to or attainment of motives."[8] Confirming those beliefs we like and disconfirming those we don't are examples of motivated reasoning.

Even when we think we are reasoning logically, we can fall into several kinds of reasoning errors. Here are five examples:[9]

1. Abductive Reasoning (sometimes called affirming the consequent): The general form is to conclude P from the two propositions, "IF P THEN Q" and Q. Although abductive reasoning may lead to good guesses, it is not guaranteed to produce valid conclusions. For example, from the proposition "if it rained last night, the grass will be wet in the morning," and "the grass is wet this morning," one might be tempted to conclude "it rained last night." But, of course, there may be other reasons why the grass is wet, so the conclusion isn't guaranteed. Abductive reasoning

can often lead to useful hypotheses, but such hypotheses aren't necessarily valid.

2. Argument from Ignorance: If we have no evidence for *P*, *P* must be false. But, just because we have no evidence that Neanderthals drew cave paintings doesn't mean that they didn't. As the saying goes, "Absence of evidence is not evidence of absence."

3. False Analogy: If two entities are analogous, they share the same properties. For example, complex manmade objects are analogous to the universe, itself extremely complex. Complex artifacts are designed and built by intelligent designers, therefore the universe must also have been designed and built by an intelligent deity. Not necessarily!

4. Gambler's Fallacy: If the outcomes of a repetition of *independent* random events lean heavily toward one subset of outcomes, future repetitions will favor the other subsets. For example, if a coin toss comes up heads twenty times in a row, the next toss is more likely to be tails. Not so—it's still only a 50 percent chance for tails.

5. Post Hoc, Ergo Propter Hoc Fallacy (Latin for "after this, therefore because of this"): The general form is "*P* occurred, then *Q* occurred, therefore *P caused Q*." But, of course, some other event, say *R*, might have caused both *P* and (later) *Q*. This fallacy is very hard to avoid because it's probably part of our built-in ability to infer causation—a

very important and useful ability! It often leads to appropriate beliefs about what causes what—but not always.

There are many subjects that have caught people in belief traps of one sort or another. For example, some people believe that certain elites are trying to promote a "new world order" that would be inimical to traditional values. Others believe that government (or business or a combination of the two) is suppressing information about new medical treatments, alternative energy sources, and other useful technologies. These kinds of beliefs are examples of what are called "conspiracy theories." There are literally hundreds (if not thousands) of these, including the belief that fluoridation of water supplies is a Communist plot to take over the world and that government-sponsored vaccination programs are part of a mind-control program. Wikipedia has an extensive list.[10]

Other belief-trap subjects include intelligent design, the existence of angels, the effectiveness of water dowsing (sometimes called "witching") to locate underground water, immortality, extrasensory perception, alien abductions, flying saucers, the predictive value of dreams, and quack therapies.[11]

It's interesting to speculate about how some of these beliefs would fare if subjected to a process I call "belief expansion." By that I mean the elaboration of a belief by filling it out with related beliefs. Belief expansion is analogous to the efforts of scientists to expand their theories. When scientific theories are first proposed, they are always in need of elaboration. For example, when Niels Bohr worked out his model of the atom in which "planetary" electrons revolved around a central nucleus, it remained to describe the properties and orbits of the electrons (among other things).

A similar process can be applied to beliefs. For example, take the belief in water dowsing. If dowsing with a wooden stick helps find underground water, how do various properties of the stick affect performance as those properties are gradually varied? What about its composition and size—does it have to be at least as big as x and no bigger than y? How exactly does performance degrade as it approaches these limits? What about the stick's density and color? And if answers to these questions are offered, what's the explanation for how these dowsing-stick properties act to affect performance?

As another example, take the belief that people have immortal souls that survive death. The process of belief expansion might involve asking (among other things) whether our close cousins the Neanderthals had souls, and (for that matter) if all animals have souls. The process of attempting to expand a belief can present difficult (and unwanted) challenges to those who hold it.

For many of us, it doesn't matter too much what we believe about some of these subjects. For example, unless you are in the well-digging business, you probably don't need to take a position on dowsing. And belief in personal angels is probably harmless unless it encourages you to behave recklessly, counting on angels to intercede if needed.

To be effective parents or citizens though, or for our personal well-being, what we believe about many things does matter. Our views on evolution might affect how we vote in a school board election. That almost half of all Americans don't believe in evolution (according to a 2012 Gallup Poll) is depressing. What does that say about our ability to teach and communicate science—a subject so critical to our progress, health, and prosperity? Our beliefs about global warming might affect our support for alternative sources of energy. Our beliefs about the effects of media violence on young children might affect what we permit our children to watch on TV. And, on and on. Fortunately, we are able to look at our beliefs and make modifications to them so they can serve us better.

In conclusion, this book has been about my *meta-beliefs*, that is to say, my beliefs about beliefs. One of them is that our only portal for obtaining information about the "world out there" is through our limited and error-prone sensory apparatus (both natural and invented). It's as if we were separated from reality itself by a translucent and foggy "sensory curtain," impervious to everything except whatever sensory data can find their way through. Our perceptual systems, using existing beliefs and expectations,

To be effective parents or citizens though, or for our personal well-being, what we believe about many things does matter.

then convert what comes through the window to beliefs that help us to function effectively in the reality within which we are embedded.

Another one of my meta-beliefs is that the scientific method offers the best way discovered so far to invent and evaluate beliefs. There are people who claim that science is "just one way to know," yielding knowledge not necessarily better than their own intuitions, inner feelings, and revelations. But "these other ways" have not produced models of reality that can compete with those produced by science—models that have given modern societies unprecedented understanding of and control over the natural world.

Probably the best antidote to belief traps is to expose our beliefs to the reasoned criticisms of others, just as scientists do. As the philosopher John Stuart Mill wrote, "[the person who] has sought for objections and difficulties, instead of avoiding them, and has shut out no light which can be thrown upon the subject from any quarter ... has a right to think his judgment better than that of any person, or any multitude, who have not gone through a similar process."[12]

Note: Some of the definitions given here are based on the way I use these words in this book and may vary from conventional definitions. Italicized words can be cross-referenced in the glossary.

abduction
A guess that the antecedent of an implication may be true given its consequent. That is, using the proposition IF *P* THEN *Q*, and *Q*, guess *P*.

aether
A hypothesized substance in space once thought to be required for the propagation of electromagnetic waves.

antecedent
In logic, the IF term of an IF-THEN statement.

Bayesian belief network
A network of propositions, each having links to other propositions, and each having a probability value that affects the values of other propositions in the network through the links.

belief
A proposition that one holds with a strength that could be very weak, very strong, or anything in-between.

belief expansion
The process of adding beliefs related to a given belief.

causality
A relation between two events in which one causes another.

causality reasoning
The process by which the likelihood of one proposition is changed given another proposition that helps to cause it. (The opposite of *evidential reasoning*.)

coherence theories of truth
Philosophical definitions of truth that involve relationships (such as consistency) among other propositions.

computer system
A computer together with a program.

confirmation bias
The tendency to give added weight to evidence that supports a belief already held.

consequence
A conclusion derived through logic or one that is an effect of a cause.

consequent
In logic, the THEN term of an IF-THEN statement

consilience
The property of a unifying theory that subsumes or explains a number of other theories.

correspondence theories of truth
Philosophical definitions of truth that involve relationships between propositions about reality and reality itself.

critical thinking
The process of examining a proposition in detail, taking into account the influences of as many related propositions as possible.

declarative knowledge
Knowledge that can be expressed by declarative sentences. (Contrast with *procedural knowledge*.)

disconfirmation bias
The tendency to give less weight to evidence that undermines a belief already held.

entities
Parameters of a theory that can be adjusted as needed to make the theory a better fit with the data that the theory is supposed to describe.

epicycle
Small circular orbits superimposed on larger orbits, as in the Ptolemaic or geocentric theory.

evidential reasoning
The process by which the likelihood of one proposition is changed given another proposition it causes. (The opposite of *causality reasoning*.)

exhaustive events
A set of events at least one of which occurs.

expert
Someone who is particularly knowledgeable about a certain subject or subjects. One who has studied the subject in detail.

explaining away
Diminishing belief in one cause because of enhanced belief in an alternative cause.

explanation
A set of statements from which another statement follows or is made highly probable.

explanationism
The process of finding an explanatory theory for a statement or theory (usually called *reductionism*).

explanatory power
The ability of a theory to explain a wide range of other theories.

fact
A statement that is believed very, very strongly.

falsifiability
The possibility that future experiments testing a theory might greatly diminish belief in it.

fast versus slow thinking
The processes of reaching conclusions based on habitual, automatic responses versus those based on thorough and analytic deliberation.

frontier science
Science that is highly speculative or newly proposed and has not gained universal acceptance among experts.

gambler's fallacy
The idea that the probabilities of future independent events are influenced by the outcomes of past events.

instrumentalism
The philosophical view that knowledge should be judged by its usefulness, such as its ability to make accurate predictions.

Intergovernmental Panel on Climate Change (IPCC)
A group of experts on possible climate change and its causes.

intuition
The process of arriving at a conclusion based on inner feelings.

knobs on a theory
See *entities*.

know
A word used for a belief that is held very, very strongly.

knowledge
The sum total of one's information about a subject or subjects.

logical deduction
A conclusion arrived at by logical inference.

model
A symbolic description that can be used to predict and understand phenomena. Examples include a set of beliefs about the phenomena and computer simulations of it.

mutually exclusive events
A set of events only one of which can occur.

network
A structure consisting of nodes and links between them.

objectivity
The quality of being independent of personal, subjective bias.

Occam's razor
See *parsimony*.

odds
A ratio of the probability of an event to 1 minus the probability of that event.

parimutuel system
A system for calculating probabilities (or odds) of events as bets are placed on those events.

parsimony
A bias favoring the simplest explanation.

probability
A measure of the likelihood of an event or proposition.

procedural knowledge
Knowledge about a routine that is built into the routine itself. (Contrast with *declarative knowledge*.)

reality
The world in which we are embedded and which we can sense aspects of, and which we can affect.

reductionism
The process of finding an explanatory theory for a statement or theory (also called called *explanationism*).

relativism
The philosophical view that the validity of beliefs is relative to the person or persons holding them.

robot
A mechanical contrivance with sensors and effectors controlled by a computer system.

scientific method
An informal process of inquiry, debate, and validation used by scientists to develop and test theories about the natural world.

scientific theory
A theory about the natural world that is consistent with the results of experiments designed to test it, that makes predictions about the results of other experiments, and is falsifiable.

semantic network
A network displaying the relationships between individuals, classes of individuals, and their properties.

simulation
A computer program that is a model of some phenomenon or phenomena.

strength of a belief
A measure of one's confidence in a belief.

theory
An explanation for observed data or for another theory.

truth
A belief having a very, very high strength.

virtual reality
A model of reality.

Watson
The IBM computer program famous for competing on the TV program *Jeopardy!*

NOTES

Opening Epigraphs

1. Quotation taken from Louis Menand, *The Metaphysical Club: A Story of Ideas in America* (New York: Farrar, Straus and Giroux, 2001), p. 225.

2. W. H. Auden, as quoted in "The Double Man," by Adam Gopnik in *The New Yorker*, Sept. 23, 2002, p. 91. Originally from W. H. Auden, "Effective Democracy," *Booksellers Quarterly*, 1939, reprinted in *The Complete Works of W. H. Auden: Prose, Volume II, 1939–1948*, ed. E. Mendelson (Princeton: Princeton University Press, 2002).

Chapter 1

1. Other types of knowledge include episodic knowledge, place knowledge, and visual and auditory knowledge. We are mainly concerned here with declarative knowledge, the kind we use to represent beliefs.

2. Karl Popper, "The Rationality of Scientific Revolutions: Selection *Versus* Instruction," in *The Myth of the Framework: In Defense of Science and Rationality*, ed. M. A. Notturno (New York: Routledge, 1994), p. 7.

3. David Deutsch, *The Fabric of Reality* (London: Penguin Books, 1997), p. 121.

4. Richard Dawkins, *Unweaving the Rainbow: Science, Delusion, and the Appetite for Wonder* (Boston: Houghton Mifflin, 1998), pp. 275–276.

Chapter 2

1. Daniel Kahneman, *Thinking, Fast and Slow* (New York: Farrar, Straus and Giroux, 2011).

2. Richard Dawkins, *Unweaving the Rainbow: Science, Delusion and the Appetite for Wonder* (New York: Houghton Mifflin Company, 1998).

3. From the lyrics of "Munchhausen" by Friedrich Hollaender. English lyrics by Jeremy Lawrence from a translation by Alan Lareau; from the printed matter of the London CD *Ute Lemper, Berlin Cabaret Songs* (452 849–2).

4. Robin Hanson, private communication, 1999.

Chapter 3

1. David W. Fleck, "Evidentiality and Double Tense in Matses," *Language* 83, no. 3 (2007): 589–614.

2. Jerome Bruner and Leo Postman, "On the Perception of Incongruity: A Paradigm," *Journal of Personality* 18, no. 2 (December 1949): 206–223.

3. "New Jersey Court Issues Guidance for Juries About Reliability of Eyewitnesses," *New York Times*, July 19, 2012, A16.

4. Paul McCartney, "The Fool on the Hill" (lyrics to song), 1967.

5. For an interesting book about this kind of childhood reasoning, see Alison Gopnik, Andrew N. Meltzoff, and Patricia K. Kuhl, *The Scientist in the Crib: What Early Learning Tells Us About the Mind* (New York: HarperCollins, 2000).

Chapter 4

1. Samuel Arbesman, *The Half-life of Facts: Why Everything We Know Has an Expiration Date*, New York: Penguin Group, 2012.

2. The IPCC website is available at http://www.ipcc.ch/organization/organization.shtml.

3. All IPPC reports are available at http://www.ipcc.ch/publications_and_data/publications_and_data_reports.shtml.

4. A report of Working Group I of the Intergovernmental Panel on Climate Change Summary for Policymakers, available at http://www.ipcc.ch/pdf/assessment-report/ar4/wg1/ar4-wg1-spm.pdf. Their fifth report is due to be released in 2014. A draft of that report cites even stronger evidence for anthropogenic global warming.

5. "Global Climate Change: NASA's Eyes on Earth," available at http://climate.nasa.gov/evidence.

6. Richard A. Muller, "The Conversion of a Climate-Change Skeptic," *The New York Times*, July 30, 2012, A19.

7. Bertrand Russell, "On the Value of Scepticism," from *The Will to Doubt* (New York: Philosophical Library, 1958).

8. One can also look at the IPCC reports for more detailed discussions of the evidence for the consequences of global warming.

9. "Volcanic Gases and Climate Change Overview," USGS Volcano Hazards Program, available at http://volcanoes.usgs.gov/hazards/gas/climate.php.

10. Karl Popper, *The World of Parmenides: Essays on the Presocratic Enlightenment*, "Essay 1, The World of Parmenides," (New York: Routledge, 1998), p. 26.

Chapter 5

1. The author Louis Menand wrote, "[The pragmatists] Holmes, James, Peirce, and Dewey … said repeatedly [that beliefs] are just bets on the future." Louis Menand, *The Metaphysical Club: A Story of Ideas in America*, (New York: Farrar, Straus and Giroux, 2001), p. 440.

2. USGS Working Group on California Earthquake Probabilities, "Earthquake Probabilities in the San Francisco Bay Region: 2000 to 2030—A Summary of Findings," available at http://geopubs.wr.usgs.gov/open-file/of99-517/#_Toc464419657.

3. The websites of these markets are, respectively: http://tippie.uiowa.edu/
iem, http://www.ideosphere.com/fx-bin/ListClaims and http://www.hsx.com.
4. See *Abrams v. United States*, 250 U.S. 616,630 (1919).

Chapter 6

1. Drew Khlentzos, "Semantic Challenges to Realism," *The Stanford Encyclopedia of Philosophy* (Winter 2004 edition), Edward N. Zalta, ed., available at http://plato.stanford.edu/archives/win2004/entries/realism-sem-challenge.
2. Hilary Putnam, *Reason, Truth, and History* (Cambridge: Cambridge University Press, 1981), p. 52.
3. Louis Menand, *The Metaphysical Club: A Story of Ideas in America* (New York: Farrar, Straus and Giroux, 2001), p. 363.
4. As quoted by Aage Petersen in "The Philosophy of Niels Bohr," *Bulletin of the Atomic Scientists* 19, no. 7 (September 1963).
5. Robert Bruce Lindsay and Henry Margenau, *Foundations of Physics* (Woodbridge, CT: Ox Bow Press, 1981), p 1. (My thanks to Sidney Liebes for pointing out this quotation.)
6. Richard Rorty, "Being that can be understood is language," Richard Rorty on H.-G. Gadamer, *London Review of Books* 22, no. 6 (March 16, 2000).
7. Richard Rorty, "Pragmatism, Relativism, and Irrationalism," Presidential Address, *Proceedings and Addresses of the American Philosophical Association* 53, no. 6 (August, 1980): 719–738, available at http://www.jstor.org/discover/10.2307/3131427?uid=3739696&uid=2&uid=4&uid=3739256&sid=21103031110243.

Chapter 7

1. Albert Einstein, "Physics and Reality," 1936, reprinted in *Ideas and Opinions* (New York: Crown Publishing Company, 1954), p. 290.
2. Rosanna Gorini, "Al-Haytham the Man of Experience, First Steps in the Science of Vision," *Journal of the International Society for the History of Islamic Medicine* 2, no. 4 (2003): 53–55, available at http://www.ishim.net/ishimj/4/10.pdf.
3. Karl R. Popper, *The Logic of Scientific Discovery*, Chapter IV, originally published in 1959 (New York: Routledge, 2000).
4. Brian Greene, *The Elegant Universe: Superstrings, Hidden Dimensions, and the Quest for the Ultimate Theory* (New York: Norton, 1999).
5. Arthur Koestler used the term "sleepwalkers" in his book about the development of cosmological theories. See Arthur Koestler, *The Sleepwalkers: A History of Man's Changing Vision of the Universe* (New York: MacMillan, 1959).
6. François Jacob, "The Birth of the Operon," *Science* 332 (May 2011): 767.

7. James Clerk Maxwell, "A dynamical theory of the electromagnetic field," *Philosophical Transactions of the Royal Society of London* 155 (1865): 459–512.

8. More information about Crookes tubes is available at http://en.wikipedia .org/wiki/Crookes_tube.

9. Joyce Appleby, Lynn Hunt, and Margaret Jacob, *Telling the Truth About History* (New York: W. W. Norton & Co., 1994), p. 195.

10. Michael Polanyi, *Personal Knowledge: Toward a Post-Critical Philosophy* (Chicago: The University of Chicago Press, 1958), p. 18.

11. Technical underpinnings for this claim involve what statisticians call "the bias-variance tradeoff."

12. Quotation from *Popper Selections*, ed. David Miller (Princeton, NJ: Princeton University Press, 1985), p. 119.

13. See http://www.nasa.gov/mission_pages/gpb/gpb_results.html for details about Gravity Probe B.

14. David Miller, "Sokal & Bricmont: Back to the Frying Pan," *Pli 9* (2000): 156–73.

15. Edward O. Wilson, *Consilience: The Unity of Knowledge* (New York: Alfred A. Knopf, 1998), p. 52.

16. Ibid., p. 59.

17. Thomas S. Kuhn, *The Structure of Scientific Revolutions* (Chicago: The University of Chicago Press, 1962).

18. Paul Feyerabend, *Against Method* (London: Verso, 1995).

Chapter 8

1. The Google blog about self-driving automobiles is available at http:// googleblog.blogspot.com/2010/10/what-were-driving-at.html.

2. Daniel Dennett, *The Intentional Stance* (Cambridge, MA: Bradford Books, 1989).

3. John McCarthy, "Ascribing Mental Qualities to Machines," in *Formalizing Common Sense: Papers by John McCarthy*, ed. Vladimir Lifschitz (Norwood, NJ: Ablex Publishing Company, 1990), p. 104.

4. See, for example, Oren Etzioni et al., "Open Information Extraction: the Second Generation," *Proceedings of the Twenty-Second International Joint Conference on Artificial Intelligence*, Vol. 1, pp. 3–10, 2011.

5. Eric Horvitz et al., "Prediction, Expectation, and Surprise: Methods, Designs, and Study of a Deployed Traffic Forecasting Service," *Proceedings of Uncertainty in Artificial Intelligence*, 2005, pp. 275–283.

6. Aude G. Billard and D. Grollman, "Robot Learning by Demonstration," Scholarpedia 2, no. 12 (2013): 3824. See http://www.scholarpedia.org/article/ Robot_learning_by_demonstration.

7. Pieter Abbeel et al., "An Application of Reinforcement Learning to Aerobatic Helicopter Flight," in *Advances in Neural Information Processing Systems*, Vol. 19, ed. B. Schölkopf, J. Platt, and T. Hoffman (Cambridge, MA: The MIT Press, 2007), pp. 1–8.

Chapter 9

1. Cass R. Sunstein, *Going to Extremes: How Like Minds Unite and Divide* (New York: Oxford University Press, 2009).

2. From a summary on the back cover of Sunstein's book.

3. Eli Pariser, *The Filter Bubble: What the Internet Is Hiding from You* (New York: The Penguin Press, 2011).

4. Daniel T. Gilbert, "How Mental Systems Believe," *American Psychologist* 46, no. 2 (February 1991): 107–119.

5. From Feynman's interview with *Nova*, January 25, 1983.

6. Cass R. Sunstein, "Breaking Up the Echo," *New York Times*, September 18, 2012, A25.

7. From the website, available at http://www.psychologytoday.com/blog/happiness-in-world/201104/the-two-kinds-belief.

8. Drew Westen et al., "Neural Bases of Motivated Reasoning: An fMRI Study of Emotional Constraints on Partisan Political Judgment in the 2004 U.S. Presidential Election," *Journal of Cognitive Neuroscience* 18, no. 11 (2006): 1947–1958.

9. For an extensive list of reasoning errors, see http://en.wikipedia.org/wiki/List_of_fallacies.

10. For a list of conspiracy theories compiled by Wikipedia, see http://en.wikipedia.org/wiki/List_of_conspiracy_theories.

11. Several authors have written about many of these pseudoscientific beliefs. See Michael Shermer, *Why People Believe Weird Things: Pseudoscience, Superstition, and Other Confusions of Our Time* (New York: Henry Holt and Company, 1997); Michael Shermer, *The Believing Brain: From Ghosts and Gods to Politics and Conspiracies, How We Construct Beliefs and Reinforce Them as Truths* (New York: Times Books, 2011); Robert Park, *Voodoo Science: The Road from Foolishness to Fraud* (New York: Oxford University Press, 2000); and Robert Todd Carroll, *The Skeptics Dictionary: A Collection of Strange Beliefs, Amusing Deceptions and Dangerous Delusions* (New York: John Wiley & Sons, 2003).

12. John Stuart Mill, *On Liberty*, London: J. W. Parker, 1859. Reprinted in Kathy Casey (ed.), John Stuart Mill, *On Liberty* (Mineola, NY: Dover Publications, 2002).

FURTHER READINGS

Carroll, Robert Todd. *The Skeptic's Dictionary: A Collection of Strange Beliefs, Amusing Deceptions and Dangerous Delusions.* New York: John Wiley & Sons, 2003.

Deutsch, David. *The Fabric of Reality.* London: Penguin Books, 1997.

Feyerabend, Paul. *Against Method.* London: Verso, 1995.

Feynman, Richard P. *The Meaning of It All: Thoughts of a Citizen-Scientist.* [Based on a three-part public lecture Feynman gave at the University of Washington in 1963.] Jackson, TN: Perseus Books, 1998.

Kahneman, Daniel. *Thinking, Fast and Slow.* New York: Farrar, Straus and Giroux, 2011.

Kuhn, Thomas S. *The Structure of Scientific Revolutions.* Chicago: The University of Chicago Press, 1962.

Nørretranders, Tor. *The User Illusion: Cutting Consciousness Down to Size.* English Translation Version. New York: Penguin Books, 1998.

Polanyi, Michael. *Personal Knowledge: Towards a Post-Critical Philosophy.* Chicago: The University of Chicago Press, 1958.

Quine, Willard Van Orman and Joseph S. Ullian, *The Web of Belief.* Second Edition. New York: Random House, 1978.

Russell, Bertrand. "On the Value of Scepticism," from *The Will to Doubt.* New York: Philosophical Library, 1958.

Shermer, Michael. *Why People Believe Weird Things: Pseudoscience, Superstition, and Other Confusions of Our Time.* New York: Henry Holt and Company, 1997.

Shermer, Michael. *The Believing Brain: From Ghosts and Gods to Politics and Conspiracies, How We Construct Beliefs and Reinforce Them as Truths.* New York: Times Books, 2011.

INDEX

Abductive reasoning, 61, 123
Absolute truths, 70–71
Aether, 89–90
Al-Haytham, 75–76, 141
Alien abduction, 31, 125
Ampère, André-Marie, 87, 99
Angels, 18, 31, 125, 127
Appleby, Joyce, 94, 142
Arbesman, Sam, 36, 140
Argument from ignorance, 124
Aristarchus of Samos, 96
Assessment, as a stage in processing
    new information, 118, 120–121

Bacon, Francis, 76
Bacon, Roger, 76
Bayes, Thomas, 61
Bayesian belief networks, 58–61, 70
Bayes' rule, 61
Beatles, 24, 140
Beliefs, 1–2
  analogy with clothes, 20
  as bets, 53, 55, 140
  coherence of, 48, 69–70
  competition among, 47, 57
  consequences of, xiii, 12, 22,
      27–28, 37–38, 41–44, 47, 50, 59,
      73, 102, 116
  as descriptions of reality, 7, 66
  effects of lifestyle on, 117–118
  expansion of, 125–126
  of experts, 37, 40–41, 50, 57, 102,
      122
  explanations for, 14, 16, 22, 27–33
  hierarchy of, 16

  as knowledge, xii, 1
  as mental constructions, 27–28
  networks of, 43–44, 47–48, 57–62,
      70, 113
  of parents, 21, 37
  of robots and computers, 105–116
  scientific, 16–17, 76–78, 81, 83
  strengths of, xiii, 35–36, 43, 48,
      51–52, 73, 117, 122
  of teachers, 26, 37
  tentativeness of, 3–4, 117
  their sources, 21–33
  their use by professionals, 11
  updating those of computers, 110,
      112–113
  uses of, 11, 20
  of Watson, the IBM computer,
      106, 108–109
Big Bang, 17, 33, 77, 86
Bohr, Niels, 66, 77, 92, 126, 141
Boldness, of theories, 96, 99–100
Brahe, Tycho, 96–97
Bruner, Jerome, 22, 140

Cathode rays, 88–89
Causality reasoning, 58, 62–63
Cause, 16
  due to superstition, 30–31
  of global warming, 40, 42, 58, 62
  of medical symptoms, 46
  of perceptual errors, 24
Clearflow, 113
Climate change. See Global warming
Cognitive scientists, xi, 3, 5
Coherence of beliefs, 48, 70

Coherence theory of truth, 69
Cold fusion, 95, 100
Comprehension, as a stage in
    processing new information,
    118, 120
Computer and robot beliefs,
    105–116
Computer simulations, 7, 79
Concepts
  as building blocks for explana-
    tions, 31–32
  as building blocks for scientific
    theories, 78–79
  invention of, 66–67, 69
Confirmation bias, 121–122
Consequences
  of actions evoked by beliefs, xiii,
    12, 122
  of beliefs, 22, 27–28, 41–44, 46,
    50, 59, 73, 102, 116
  of global warming, 41–42, 62, 140
  of theories, 47
Consilient theories, 98–99, 142
Conspiracy theories, 125, 143–145
Contraction effects in special relativ-
    ity, 91
Copernicus, Nicholas, 96
Correspondence theory of truth,
    67, 69
Credo consolans, 18
Critical discussion
  importance of, 7, 94, 100, 129
  its principal advantage, 48
  of theories, 7, 48, 84, 93–94, 100,
    102
Critical thinking, elements of,
    37–46, 48–50, 75
Criticism. See Critical discussion
Crookes tubes, 88–89

Dawkins, Richard, 8, 18, 139
Day science, 85
Declarative knowledge, xi–xii, 3, 5,
    7, 107–108, 113, 116, 139
Dennett, Daniel, 106, 142
Descartes, René, 76
Descriptions of reality, 24, 50,
    65–68, 75, 77–78, 85, 97
Deutsch, David, 7–8, 139, 145
Dirac, Paul, 92
Disconfirmation bias, 121–122
DNA, xi, 17–18, 77
Dowsing, 125–127
Dreams, predictive value of, 64, 125

Einstein, Albert, 17, 75, 82, 91, 99,
    141
  his general theory of relativity, 33,
    82, 99
  his special theory of relativity,
    91, 99
Electrodynamics, 98
Electromagnetic force field, 88, 142
Electromagnetic waves
  history of knowledge about, 86–91
  propagation of, 88, 90
  speed of, 82, 88, 90–91
  theories about, 86, 88, 91, 142
Electromagnetism, discovery of,
    87–88
Electrons, their discovery, 89
Elliptical orbits of planets, 16, 96
Entanglement, in quantum mechan-
    ics, 93
Entities, number of in a theory,
    96–97
Epicycles, 96–97
Equivalence of mass and energy, as
    predicted by special relativity, 91

Errors
  by eyewitnesses, 23, 140
  in perceiving playing cards, 22–23
  perceptual, 23–24
  of reasoning, 123–125
ESP. *See* Extrasensory perception
Eternal truths, 22, 26
Evidential reasoning, 61–63
Exhaustive probabilities, 52–53
Expansion of beliefs, 126
Experts
  on accepting their opinions,
    39–41, 50
  beliefs of, 39, 40–41, 50, 57, 102,
    122
  estimating odds by, 53–54, 56
  opinions of regarding global warm-
    ing, 39–40
Explaining away, 45–46, 62–63
Explanationism, 17
Explanations, xi, 14, 16–17, 22,
    27–33
  for beliefs, 22, 27–33, 41–46, 50,
    59, 73, 116
  for global warming, 42–46
  materials used in, 31–32, 92
Explanatory power of theories, 95,
    97–98
Extrasensory perception, 2, 31, 81,
    95, 125
Extrasensory ways of perceiving,
    26–27
Eyewitness errors, 23, 140

Facebook, its effects on beliefs, 118
Facts, 35–36
  half-life of, 36, 140
  as part of scientific knowledge, 76,
    78–80

False analogy, 124
Falsifiability of scientific theories,
    79–83
Faraday, Michael, 88, 99
Fast and slow thinking, 13, 37, 46,
    139, 145
Feyerabend, Paul, 101–102, 142,
    145
Feynman, Richard, 18, 120, 143, 145
Filter bubble, 118, 143
Fleck, David, 21, 139
Fleischmann, Martin, 95, 100
Flying saucers, 125
Foci of planetary orbits, 97
Fodor, Jerry, 3
Franklin, Benjamin, 87
Frequency method, 54
Frontier science, 77, 84, 122

Galileo, 67–68, 76, 78
Gambler's fallacy, 124
Gilbert, Daniel T., 118, 120, 143
Global warming, 37–46, 57–59,
    61–62, 98, 127, 140
  example of critical thinking, 37–46
Goldstein, Eugen, 88
Google
  its effects on beliefs, 118
  its self-driving automobiles,
    105–106, 108, 110
Gravity Probe B, 99, 142
Grosseteste, Robert, 76

Habits, their role in controlling ac-
    tions, 12–13
Hanson, Robin, 20, 139
Heisenberg, Werner, 92
Heliocentric theory, 67, 96
Hittorf, Johann, 88

Holmes, Oliver Wendell, Jr., 57, 140
Hunt, Lynn, 94, 142

Illusions, 18
   visual, 23–25
Immortality, 81, 125–126
Inconsistency
   of beliefs, 69, 123
   of scientific theories, 82, 84, 92
Infrared light, discovery of, 87
Instrumentalism, the philosophical
      doctrine of, 73
Intelligent design, 47, 124–125
Intergovernmental Panel on Climate
      Change (IPCC), 39–41, 140
Intuition, 37–38, 85, 129

Jacob, François, 85, 142
Jacob, Margaret, 94, 142
JamBayes, a traffic prediction
      system, 113
Jeopardy! and Watson, the IBM
      computer, 106, 108–109

Kahneman,Daniel,13,37,46,139,145
Keats, John, 18
Kepler, Johannes, 96–97
Knobs on a theory, 81, 97
Know (its use as a word), v, xi, xiii, 2,
      35–36, 72–73
Knowledge
   declarative, xi–xii, 3, 5, 7,
      108–111, 139
   procedural, xi, 5, 12, 113
   production of, 84–85
   as represented in Bayesian net-
      works, 58–59
   of robots and computer programs,
      xi, 107–114

scientific, xii, 2, 76–78, 84
   as awe inspiring, 18
   its evolution regarding electro-
      magnetic waves, 86–92
   of the world, xii, 1, 5, 8, 14, 101,
      127
Kuhn, Thomas, 101, 142, 145

Learning, 110
   by demonstration, 113, 143
   reinforcement, 114, 143
Lifestyle, its effects on beliefs,
      117–118
Light, wave or particle, 92
Lindsay, Robert, 67, 141
Logical reasoning, 27, 29, 122–123
Lorentz, Hendrik, 91

Machine learning, 110
Magnetism, 87
Margenau, Henry, 67, 141
Markets (electronic)
   examples of, 57, 141
   use of to estimate probabilities,
      55–57
Mathematical truths, 70, 72
   direct perception of, 26–27
Maxwell, James Clerk, 88, 91, 98,
      142
McCarthy, John, 107, 142
Menand, Louis, v, 66, 139, 140, 141
Mentalese, 3
Meta-beliefs, 72, 127, 129
Michelson, Albert, 90, 95
Michelson-Morley experiment, 90
Mill, John Stuart, 129, 144
Models
   components of, 7, 69
   as constructions, 92

our need to build, 31
of reality, 7, 9, 65–66, 69, 73, 129
use of by robots, 110
used by visual perception, 23
Morley, Edward, 90, 95
Motivated reasoning, 123, 143
Muller, Richard A., 40, 140
Mutually exclusive probabilities, 52–53
Mythology, 16

Networks
  Bayesian belief, 57–62, 70
  of beliefs, 43–44, 47–48
  semantic, 108, 110–111
Newton, Isaac, 17, 76, 78, 86
  his gravitational theory, 17, 82, 98
Night science, 85

Objectivity in science, 85, 94
Objects, invention of, 22, 31, 65–66, 69
Objects, properties, and relations
  as components of our models, 7, 31, 69
  independent existence of, 65–66
  as part of reality, 7
  as part of scientific knowledge, 76–77
Occam, William of, 96
Odds as a way of expressing probabilities, 53
Ontologies, 110
Ørsted, Hans Christian, 87

Paradigm shift, 101
Parameters of a theory, 80–81
Paranoia, 26
Parents, beliefs of, 21, 37

Parimutuel system, 55
Pariser, Eli, 118, 143
Parsimony of theories, 64, 95–97
Pattern recognition, and its use in selecting actions, 13
Penrose, Roger, 26
Photons, 91–92
Planck, Max, 91
Plato, 22
Pons, Stanley, 95, 100
Popper, Karl, 7, 48, 82, 99, 139, 140, 141
Postdictions, 86
Post hoc, ergo proper hoc fallacy, 124
Postman, Leo, 22
Predictions
  role of beliefs in making, 11
  their role in evaluating beliefs, 47, 73, 79, 95, 99
Probabilities, 51–64
  estimating their values by markets, 55–56
  expressed as odds, 53
  frequency method for estimating values of, 54
  subjective, 54–56
Procedural knowledge, xi, 5, 12, 113
Ptolemaic theory, 96–97, 101
Putnam, Hilary, 66, 141

Quack therapies, 125
Quanta, 91
Quantum mechanics, 2, 17, 33, 77, 82, 84, 86, 92–93, 101

Realism, the philosophical doctrine of, 65–66, 141
Reality, xii, 7–9

descriptions of, 24, 50, 65–68, 75, 77–78, 85, 97
its existence, 65
its impact, 65
models of, 7, 9, 65–66, 69, 73, 129
virtual, 7–9
Reasoning errors, 123–125
Reasoning processes, their role in beliefs, 122–123
Reductionism, 17
Reinforcement learning, 114, 143
Relational databases, 108
Relativism, the philosophical doctrine of, 73, 141
Relativity
general theory of, 33, 82, 99
special theory of, 91, 99
Ritter, Johann Wilhelm, 87
Robot and computer beliefs, 105–116
Röntgen, Wilhelm, 89
Rorty, Richard, 70, 73, 141
Russell, Bertrand, 40–41, 140, 145

Schrödinger, Erwin, 92
Science, viewed as similar to solving jigsaw puzzles, 84–85
Scientific beliefs, 16–17, 76–78, 81, 83
Scientific knowledge, xii, 2, 76–79, 84
as awe inspiring, 18
its evolution regarding electromagnetic waves, 86–92
production of, 84–85
Scientific method, xiv, 47, 75–86
use of for evaluating beliefs, 102
Scientific theories, 2, 17, 47, 76, 78–79, 81–82, 84, 126

Scientists
how they evaluate theories, 47
their skepticism, 37
Selecting actions, role of beliefs in, xiii, 11
Self-driving automobiles, 105–106, 110
Semantic networks, 110–111
Sentences
declarative, xii, 3, 107, 116
for stating beliefs, 2, 5, 35, 65, 108, 116
Shakey the Robot, 107
Shepard, Roger, 24
Simulations
computer, 7, 79
as scientific theories, 79
Slow thinking. See Fast and slow thinking
Sommerfeld, Arnold, 92
Speed of light, 82, 88, 90–91
Strengths, of beliefs, xiii, 35–36, 43, 48, 51–52, 73, 117, 122,
String theory, 17, 84
Subjective probability, 54–56
Sunstein, Cass R., 118, 121, 143
Superposition, in quantum mechanics, 93
Superstitions, 30–31, 125–126
Systems 1 and 2, 13

Teachers, beliefs of, 26, 37
Textbook knowledge, 77, 80, 82
Theories
about past events, 86
bold, 96, 99–100
consistency of, 82
conspiracy, 125
criticism of, 7, 48, 84, 93–94, 100, 102

expansion of, 126
explanatory power of, 95, 97–98
falsifiability of, 79–83
as part of scientific knowledge,
    76–79
scientific, 2, 17, 47, 76, 78–79,
    81–82, 84, 126
simplicity of, 96–97
social and personal, xi, 2–3
Theory of everything, 84
Thinking
  elements of critical, 37–46, 48–50,
    75
  fast and slow, 13, 37, 46, 139, 145
Thompson, J. J., 89
True (its use as a word), xiii, 65, 70,
    72–73, 80
Truth
  coherence theory of, 69
  correspondence theory of, 67, 69
  philosophers' views of, 67, 69–70
Truth bell, 26

Ultraviolet light, discovery of, 87
Updating beliefs of computers, 110,
    112–113

Virtual reality, 7–9
Vision, errors and illusions of, 22–24
Visual perception, 22
Volta, Alessandro, 87

Watson, the IBM computer and
    Jeopardy!, 106, 108–109
Wilson, Edward O., 98, 100, 142
Wren, Christopher, 108–109

X–rays, 46, 78, 89